JOE LATAKGOMO

MZANSI MAGIC

Struggle, Betrayal and Glory
The Story of South African Soccer

TAFELBERG

Tafelberg,
an imprint of NB Publishers,
40 Heerengracht, Cape Town, 8001
© Joe Latakgomo (2010)

Cover design by Michelle Staples
Typesetting by Nielfa Cassiem-Carelse
Editing by Linda Pretorius
Proofreading by Glynne Newlands
Cover photograph Gallo Images
Printed in South Africa by Interpak Books, Pietermaritzburg

First edition, first impression 2010

ISBN: 978-0-624-04781-0

To my wife Angie.
Thanks for your love and understanding
during difficult times in my life.
To the memory of Ellen.

Some people think football is a matter of
life and death. I don't like that attitude.
I can assure them it is much more serious than that.

BILL SHANKLY,
former Scottish International
and former Liverpool FC manager

Contents

Foreword   11
Introduction   15
List of acronyms   19

  1. Siyavuma!   21
  2. Kick-off: The early years   37
  3. The battle for access to fields   50
  4. What's in a name?   64
  5. International betrayal   77
  6. No normal sport in an abnormal society   94
  7. Pay for play   108
  8. Bucs, Birds and Amakhosi   128
  9. The gods of football   146
10. 'The Boys'   159
11. The quest for the Cup   169

Endnotes   184

Foreword

A few months ago I read with great interest an entertaining and most informative book, *How Soccer Explains the World*, by American author Franklin Foer. It would not have been out of place if Joe Latakgomo's narration was called *How Soccer Explains South Africa*.

Football has always and will continue to evoke passion – it manifests in the intensity, violence and artistry of the game. But it is the overwhelmingly superb performances by soccer stars worldwide that has earned football the title of 'The Beautiful Game'. This aspect of the game is abundantly reflected in the lives of nearly all South Africans.

Football, generally known as soccer in our country, is deeply ingrained in our daily lives. It is a constant talking point in our media. Newspapers use soccer stories to boost their circulation figures. Politicians from opposing parties hug each other when our national or club sides achieve international glory. Sadly, nowadays the glory days seem so few and so far apart.

When political activity was suppressed by the South African apartheid regime, sport became the major forum to expose the country's racist laws. South Africa's sports isolation demoralised the country's white population to such an extent that the apartheid laws were amended to appease international opinion so that whites could be re-integrated into world sport. In effect, sport caused the first fissures in the apartheid wall.

Although soccer had its share of government collaborators, it was soccer's determination to steadfastly stand for equality that frustrated the propagators of racism in our country and its overseas supporters. Because of their support for apartheid South Africa, Sir Stanley Rous, the English President of the International Football Federation (FIFA), was ousted from this very influential position by Dr João Havelange of Brazil in 1974. This change in leadership resulted in South Africa's expulsion from FIFA in 1976.

It was organised soccer that initially challenged the government's racial legislation in a court case (which the government lost) when it tried to segregate black football into the African, Coloured and Indians groups. Although the victory was short-lived, it was a tremendous morale booster for black South Africans.

Race discrimination frustrated many of South Africa's talented black sports stars, and the only alternative was for them to seek recognition abroad. However, because of prohibitive costs, only a handful could leave the country. Most prominent were Ron Elland (representing Great Britain at the 1948 Olympic Games), Jake Ntuli (Commonwealth Boxing Champion), Precious McKenzie (representing Great Britain and New Zealand at several Olympic Games), Basil D'Oliveira (who played cricket for England), Albert Johanneson (who played football for Leeds United and was the first black person to play at Wembley in an FA Cup final), David Samaai and Jasmat Dhiraj (who won tennis tournaments abroad), to name a few.

Soccer was, and undoubtedly still is, South Africa's premier sport. It has undergone the full circle of the country's tumultuous vivacity.

Joe Latakgomo has received numerous accolades during his career as a reporter and editor for several publications, and most recently was inducted into the SAB Sports Journalists Hall of Fame. He has dodged the vilifications and violence for his forthright writing. Joe has survived and lives to tell the stories of yesteryear and the evolution of the game to where we are today. He provides us with an outstanding overview – warts and all – of the South African soccer scene, interspersed with his personal revelations of situations both controversial and profound of township activities.

It reminded me of my school days watching the games at Durban's Somtseu Road Grounds from a nearby treetop. The performance by some players after they kicked the ball or did a short dribble would make present-day stage acting look relatively mediocre.

Mzansi Magic is a must read for all soccer followers, be they fans, journalists or academics. This book will enhance the quality of anyone's bookshelf or coffee table. It is the history of South African soccer as it has never been told before.

SAM RAMSAMY
Member: International Olympic Committee
Former President: National Olympic Committee
of South Africa (NOCSA)

Introduction

The idea for this book arose from a discussion on soccer, and specifically our rough road to winning the rights to host the 2010 FIFA World Cup, following the death of former sports journalist Don Manaka.

As our discussion progressed, we realised that the story of black South African soccer has not been fully told and in a manner that is accessible to the majority of soccer fans or the easy reader. Each of us recalled a period, an event, an anecdote. We reminisced over the real Soweto derby – Moroka Swallows versus Orlando Pirates – and recalled some memorable games and colourful, larger-than-life characters. Someone mentioned the sartorially elegant Elijah 'Stetson Phansi, Stetson Phezulu' Msibi with his flashy cars; another remembered how Ewert 'The Lip' Nene, the loquacious manager and talent scout of Kaizer Chiefs, lived – and died – for soccer. Then there was Black Pirates boss, Uncle Dave Motsamai – tinker, tailor and bootleg. He demanded goals, goals and yet more goals from his players; when they lost, he would instruct the driver of his maroon luxury bus to go home and leave the players to find their own way home.

We spoke of the resilience of soccer against extreme odds: the efforts by the apartheid government to suppress the passion blacks have for soccer, the denial of facilities, and efforts to channel the energy of black soccer into their own objective of keeping blacks occupied in their spare time, fit and healthy to provide the labour that an industrialising South Africa needed at the time. We reminisced about how soccer overcame the racial and tribal barriers that the government created and how soccer actually became a mobilising force against apartheid.

The discussions were fascinating and at the end, looking at the wide-eyed interest from some of the younger people in the room, we all had the same question: why has this story not been told? And if it has to be told, who will do it? A great many of the sports journalists of the time have already passed on: Mecro Zwane, Chapman Nomtuli, Lucas Molete, Sy Mohapi, Benny Esau, Harold Pongolo, Gordon Siwani, Derrick Luthayi, Lennie Kleintjies, and now also Manaka. All of them covered sports issues and events, and their records form part of the history of South African soccer.

It is not as if the story has not been told. It has, in some form or other, but written mostly in an academic style. Previous authors have explored various aspects of the social and political economy of South Africa and particularly the impact of apartheid, both locally and internationally. Although they have researched government and municipal documents, newspapers – particularly black newspapers – and also minutes of meetings and used personal interviews, the scarcity of primary sources is evident and they have largely relied on each other and quote each other extensively in their work.

It was against this background, and cognisant of the fact that South Africa is about to host one of the greatest sporting spectacles in the world in 2010, that I accepted the challenge to make my own contribution to the record of the history of soccer in this country. The book is not intended to be an exhaustive history, but meant rather to tell the remarkable story of soccer in this country in a simple narrative that will complement existing historical accounts of the game in other contexts.

The book is based on research that includes academic papers, documents, news reports, biographies and histories of clubs and organisations. I also drew on personal notes and recollections of my time as a sports reporter and editor from the second half of the 1960s. Sections that describe our soccer culture and the passionate following by supporters intersperse the historical and political accounts to let a truly South African soccer story unfold. It is written as a narrative to allow for easy reading, and I have made every attempt to strike a balance between information from published sources, my own recollection of events, and information gleaned from various club sources. Sometimes it was impossible to reconcile the different versions of events, and details might have been filtered through the mists of time. I take full responsibility for the judgments and conclusions arrived at.

Much work still needs to be done to research the full story of not only soccer but also black sport in general. There is still many a story to be told of the blood, sweat and tears that came with sport development in this country. Hundreds have made significant contributions, and although they are not specifically mentioned in this book, I acknowledge their role. Soccer also played a significant political role: it provided the fuel for the anti-apartheid movement, the mobilisation of the masses and provided a real black economic empowerment opportunity. What I hope the book will achieve, however, is to demonstrate the role soccer has played in shaping the social fabric of the country and how its survival, despite a hostile environment, has made a positive contribution to social development.

I hope that this publication will provide as much joy to the readers as it did me in the writing, taking them on a journey with remarkable people, in remarkable circumstances, in a country whose transformation from an apartheid society to democracy is itself nothing short of a miracle. Soccer is today the most popular sport in South Africa and with the country preparing for the 2010 FIFA World Cup, I believe the publication will be timely.

I have many people to thank for seeing this project through: the publishers, for their confidence in the book; the editors, who knocked into shape what has been a hard slog of getting facts and figures, toggling between memory and other sources; Cyril McAravey, for jogging my memory on events and incidents and doing the initial edit; friends who have prodded me on when the going got tough, and of course, my wife Angie, for ensuring a writing discipline. Romeo, Bridget, Tebogo, Thabo and Refilwe – thanks for your support and understanding.

JOE LATAKGOMO

List of acronyms

ANC	African National Congress
BMSC	Bantu Men's Social Centre
BSC	Bantu Sports Club
CAF	Confederation of African Football
DDAFA	Durban and District African Football Association
DDNFA	Durban and District Native Football Association
DOCC	Donaldson Orlando Community Centre
FASA	Football Association of South Africa
FIFA	Federation of International Football Associations
FPL	Federation Professional League
IFP	Inkatha Freedom Party
JAFA	Johannesburg African Football Association
JBFA	Johannesburg Bantu Football Association
NEAD	Non-European Affairs Department
NFL	National Football League
NPSL	National Professional Soccer League
NSC	National Sports Congress
NSL	National Soccer League
PAC	Pan Africanist Congress
PSL	Premier Soccer League

SAFA	South African Football Association
SAAFA	South African African Football Association
SAB	South African Breweries
SABFA	South African Bantu Football Association
SACOS	South African Council on Sports
SAFA	South African Football Association
SANFA	South African National Football Association
SANROC	South African Non-Racial Olympic Committee
SANSL	South African National Soccer League
SASA	South African Sports Association
SASF	South African Soccer Federation
SASL	South African Soccer League
SASO	South African Students Organisation
TAFA	Transvaal African Football Association
TBFA	Transvaal Bantu Football Association
UEFA	Union of European Football Associations

1

Siyavuma![*]

It was an ordinary, uneventful Tuesday – what journalists would describe as a 'dry' day for sports stories. There was a lull in the animated conversation and the typical newsroom buzz at the *World* in Industria, a suburb west of Johannesburg.

Following a period in the late 1960s and early 1970s when there had been no structured league, soccer clubs relied heavily on the media – particularly the *World*[1] – to publicise their friendly matches. And so it was not surprising to see former Pirates official and later one of the founders of Kaizer Chiefs, Ewert 'The Lip' Nene, saunter into the sports department of the newspaper.

Everyone knew him: drivers, cleaners, printing department staff and journalists alike, not least because he was generous to a fault. He did not mind giving away a rand or two as reward for calling him 'The Lip'.

Kaizer Chiefs were scheduled to play Orlando Pirates at Orlando Stadium in Soweto the following Saturday. Chiefs had burst onto the soccer scene in 1971, bringing welcome relief to what had become a monotonous two-team race between Pirates and Moroka Swallows.

---

[*] This expression is used during consultations with a witchdoctor. The patient is expected to respond to the witchdoctor's incantations and revelations with the word *siyavuma* to indicate agreement.

Every soccer fan knew what a fixture between Pirates and Chiefs provided, and the build-up had already started. Nene boasted about the hiding Chiefs would give his former team. He declared, à la Muhammad Ali, that Chiefs would 'thump' the Bucs (short for Buccaneers, as Pirates are also known colloquially). Also, he had a secret weapon against the Buccaneers.

As he regaled the sports department with his predictions and the qualities of his players, Jimmy Sojane walked in. Sojane was an official of Orlando Pirates, a taxi owner and, by the standards of those years, a wealthy man. Cigarette in gold-plated holder dangling from the corner of his mouth, walking with an arrogant gait and head held high, he greeted Nene in a tone typical of school masters of the time, and waved to everyone in the room.

Nene shook his head, and declared: 'You see, Bra[2] Jimmy, your problem is typical of all educated people. You go to a witch-doctor in Orlando East who wears Florsheim shoes [a popular shoe label of the time]. Where have you seen a good traditional healer wearing shoes? All I have to do is get my muthi man to give a few of my supporters muthi to leave in your taxis, so that when your players get into the vehicles on Saturday, it will be all over with them!'

We could see the consternation on Sojane's face. He desperately tried to tell us that he did not believe in muthi, and laughed off Nene's threats.

But Nene had driven his psychological point home; Sojane withdrew his taxis from service for the rest of the week!

Soccer, like most things in the lives of black South Africans, is steeped in ritual and ceremony. Many black South Africans believe in ancestral spirits and the power of traditional medicine. For example, soon after birth, ceremonies to strengthen the baby and prepare the child for its first exposure to the outside world are performed. Sangomas are also called in to perform rituals to protect a household when someone falls ill or a family goes through a difficult time.

African witchcraft is believed to provide magical support to people. It has long been common for soccer teams to turn to witchcraft, or *juju* as the phenomenon is known in other parts of the continent, to gain a competitive edge. Many soccer players and fans alike will attest, if only privately, to the efficacy of potions and rituals to improve play. Clubs are known to call in witchdoctors and sangomas[3] to help them win games by casting spells on opposing teams or summoning the spirits of the ancestors to provide protection and strength.

As early as 1933, assistant editor of the black newspaper *Bantu World*, RRR Dlhomo, wrote of African teams employing traditional healers and diviners, who rubbed players' legs with muthi and made them inhale 'smoke from herbs [to] bring fear and weakness on their opponents' before a match.[4] Clubs employed these 'healers, diviners and sorcerers' to prepare for a game, with the diviners throwing bones to predict the outcome of a game.

It is known that clubs conduct cleansing ceremonies and perform rituals before important games to determine what the opposition are doing and plan a counter accordingly. Muthi is often put into soccer boots or smeared on the outfits, or uniforms are washed in potions.

Sometimes muthi is smeared on hands, and for that reason players often opt to just touch with balled fists, rather than the traditional handshake before a game. After the game, players only hug each other – particularly if it was a needle or crucial game between great rivals. And the tradition of post-match jersey exchange is not as commonplace as it is elsewhere, for fear of the opposition taking a jersey to a witchdoctor to analyse what kind of muthi had been used and from that create an antidote. There is, of course, also the other matter of the cost of soccer outfits!

Often, muthi and religious rituals are used simultaneously. Teams regularly huddle in prayer on the field before kick-off. Richard Maguire, editorial director of *Kick Off*, records in his research regarding the history of Orlando Pirates that one of the earliest patrons of the mighty Buccaneers, Bethuel Mokgosinyana, practiced pre-match rituals.[5]

'Mokgosinyana was not considered "educated" or wealthy, but his roots were deeply implanted in African culture and ubuntu,' former Pirate Sam Shabangu told Maguire.

'The patron also had "secrets"; pre-match rituals involving burning coals, fat and impenetrable smoke that would vanish at a word. On the other hand, the patron was an avid reader of the Bible and used to keep the company of priests – once quipping that if it weren't for Pirates, he would have been a priest himself,' Shabangu added.

He recalled how Mokgosinyana would take a glowing coal, put it on the ground and then place a ball of some fatty substance on the coal. In the resulting smoke, players were hardly visible and feeling teammates' shoulders would be the only sign of their presence. The players had to jump the flame on the way out. Even on the way to the stadium, often by train, players were not allowed to speak to anyone and merely had to nod acknowledgement when greeted by fans or other acquintances.

Ewert Nene didn't hesitate to admit that he used muthi and often told of team officials bumping into each other at a witchdoctor's, each denying that the purpose of their visit had anything to do with their team. A Pretoria muthi man reputedly provided services to Chiefs, Moroka Swallows and Pretoria

Callies at the same time. If two of his clients were to play each other, the team that paid better would get the stronger muthi.

Nene's antics on the field indeed often sparked riots, because fans genuinely believed that he practiced witchcraft to influence the outcome of the game. Once, ahead of a major fixture against Orlando Pirates, he declared to the media that Chiefs would field a 'mystery new player', and would only say that journalists could call him 'New man in town' for 'strategic reasons'.

On match day, the usual Chiefs players took the field – and won the game. When questioned about the matter after the game, Nene simply laughed it off and told journalists that he had actually referred to his new muthi man earlier!

Moroka Swallows' manager during the late sixties and early seventies, Sy Mthembu, always walked across the net from goalpost to goalpost and pretended to drop something at each pole. Nene had a beach towel that he would wave over the goal line before a game. Once, supporters of Pimville United Brothers (Pubs) invaded the field and snatched it from him. Pubs won the game 6–5 after being 5–1 down with about fifteen minutes left to play, perhaps the greatest comeback by any team in the history of black soccer in South Africa.

Few fans, however, noticed Pubs manager Steve Mkhasibe, sitting quietly performing his own rituals on the touchline, exhorting Chris 'Rollaway' Ndlhovu to get the ball into goal-scoring range.

Dick Phiri, the coach of Pretoria Callies during the seventies, swore by the efficacy of his muthi. He would often leave our Friday evening shebeen gathering and declare that he was 'going to Malawi' to prepare for a major game, referring to a visit to a muthi man in the township Atteridgeville. Callies opponents were so scared of the muthi that they would jump over the ground's fence to avoid using the gates, on which they believed muthi had been sprinkled to weaken their side.

Callies supporter Martin Dioke often reinforced this perception by walking onto the pitch wearing a traditional Tsonga (Shangaan) outfit and repeatedly thrusting a spear in the direction of the goalposts to indicate the number of goals Callies would score. Twice Callies beat Orlando Pirates (2–1 each time), even after the first game was abandoned because Bucs fans rioted before the final whistle.

It's not only players and club officials who rely on intervention from their ancestors; fans do too. Once, during a league match between Orlando Pirates and Black Leopards, a gale-force wind suddenly blew over advertising billboards, ripping them from their mountings. The boards hurtled across the pitch, narrowly missing players.

The referee, heeding the dangers, abandoned the game. Bucs supporters were quick to blame it on the unhappiness of the team's ancestors, with callers to a popular radio programme in the week following the incident urging Bucs chairman, Irvin Khoza, to arrange an African cleansing ritual for the team.[6]

Similarly, when Kaizer Chiefs had a bad run, their supporters often advised them to visit the grave of the legendary Ewert Nene. When Nelson 'Teenage' Dladla lost form, he was advised to go and pray and conduct rituals at Nene's grave, since Nene was killed while finalising Dladla's transfer. Years ago, when Chiefs repeatedly lost against Orlando Pirates, Nene himself accused Bucs of having buried soil from the grave of one of the most influential Orlando Pirates captains, Eric 'Scara' Sono, at the goalposts of Orlando Stadium, which, Nene believed, made it impossible for any team to beat Pirates at that venue.

The belief in witchcraft as a phenomenon is not unique to

South African soccer. In many parts of the African continent, the use of *juju* in soccer is common practice. Phyllis Martin wrote that 'Zulu religious specialists prepare teams for football matches', and in Cameroon, Sierra Leone and Liberia, 'supporters and team members perform rituals to influence results in their favour'.[7]

Already in 1950, when a team of players from the Johannesburg Bantu Football Association (JBFA) toured what was then Katanga in the Belgian Congo, the colonial authorities there banned what they described as 'superstition and fetishm' and the use of muthi and 'protective magic', according to a report in the *Bantu World*.[8] Whether or not the Katanga team did use muthi is debatable, but the JBFA team manager was convinced of it.

Vice-captain of the JBFA team, John 'American Spoon' Khoza, scored three own goals. As if that was not enough, Nonnie Moletsane added a fourth own goal, and for some strange reason, the usually reliable Zacharia 'Al die Hoekies' Mahlatsi fumbled three long shots which ended up in the back of Katanga's net. Katanga only scored one goal that was deemed a genuine attempt. The final score: JBFA XI 0, Katanga 8.

At the end of the game it was reported that the Katanga side's message to the South African team was that although their standard of football was very high, their front line refused to score.[9]

There are also many stories of a witchdoctor who has been double-crossed by a team, and the team consequently paying a heavy penalty; they would end up losing games in an unbelievable manner.

The 1992 Ivory Coast team's victory in the Africa Cup of Nations was apparently thanks to *juju* men employed by the sports minister of the country.[10] But, the story goes, when the minister failed to keep his promise of payment to the *juju* men, they put a spell on the team. For ten years the once fearsome team succumbed even to much lesser teams.

It required the intervention of the Defence and Civil Protection Minister, Moise Lida Kouassi, who reportedly pleaded with the *juju* men for forgiveness and settled the debt with a bottle of liquor and US$2 000. Whether this had anything to do with the improved performance of Ivory Coast is difficult to tell. What is fact, though, is that Ivory Coast again qualified for the World Cup.

The belief in witchcraft in African soccer persists. When Morocco made a final desperate bid to unseat South Africa from the favourite spot for hosting the 2010 FIFA World Cup, they put out a story – one of several – about South African soccer teams depending on *juju* but lacking in skill.

It is generally believed that Benin is the capital of *juju* on the continent. But, as one observer pointed out, Benin's failure to have ever made it to a World Cup is probably proof enough that muthi does not work.

Vast amounts of money are spent on muthi, but not one team will openly admit to using it. Many traditional healers are cautious when asked about the efficacy of muthi in soccer. 'Look, it depends . . .' said one when I pressed him about it. This healer, who lives on the South Africa–Swaziland border and did not want to be named, told me in an interview that a number of South African teams have used his services.

'I cannot give you names, but they include some of the top teams in the country. You must remember that it is not the muthi that wins games; the players still have to play hard. It is like buying a gun: you cannot put it on the table and expect it to defend you. You must still pull the trigger. The same applies to muthi. It is basically to protect you from those who use muthi against you,' he said.

The traditional healer emphasised the anthropological significance when he added that those who deny using muthi are denying 'their African culture and heritage'. At the same time, he acknowledged that if muthi alone were able to win games for teams, no team would spend money buying top players.

The late Force Khashane, former Orlando Pirates player, journalist and traditional healer, never hesitated when quizzed about the matter.[11] 'Yes, we used muthi during our days, and teams still use muthi today,' he said. Immaculately dressed in a grey pinstripe suit, with a piece of animal skin around his wrist, Khashane was equally comfortable attending an editorial board meeting or handing out little bottles of muthi to white staff members who had fallen victim to petty crime.

He believed the use of muthi is necessary not only to ensure a win but also for 'protection'. 'When you go into a soccer game, it is like a war. Sure, you play so that your supporters can enjoy the game, but many a player has suffered injuries that have been the result of lack of protection,' Khashane said.

Khashane recalled the early days of his own soccer career. 'We used to take our soccer boots to the clubhouse every Friday. When we were young we did not quite understand why, but we just knew that if your boots were not at the clubhouse by Friday, you would be out of the team. As young boys, we did not question this – it was the rule.'

Khashane blamed the use of foreign coaches for Bafana Bafana's woes and said they did not understand African culture and traditions. He believed Bafana's better performances were under local coaches because they all used muthi: Jomo Sono, Clive Barker and Shakes Mashaba, whose daughter incidentally is also a traditional healer.

One-time colleague of Khashane at *Pace* magazine, Cyril McAravey, says he never had any doubt that Khashane himself had 'special powers'. 'We would often have friendly wagers over the outcome of sporting events – boxing bouts or rugby, cricket or soccer matches – and I don't recall ever having won one of them.'

'Just before I left *Pace*, Force gave me a gift that I will always treasure. It was a book entitled *A Modern Herbal* and was first published in 1931. With almost 1,000 pages, it is the first complete herbal encyclopaedia ever printed and covers the use of plants and recipes of cures used by the "cunning men in English villages" dating back to the seventeenth century. It not only outlines details of the herbs' cultivation but also describes their chemical and medicinal properties. So there is no doubt that, armed with that knowledge, Force was a fundi in potions and pastes.'[12]

Many a story has been told about how white players had to adjust to the African soccer culture when they joined the black teams. South African 'Lucky' Stylianou, one of the first white players to join a black team (Kaizer Chiefs) in the 1970s, insists he never took part in the rituals. However, teammates often told how he always made sure his colleagues did. He would ask every player, 'Have you been inside?' referring to the rites performed by a muthi man in the back-room before the team left for their games.

Former AmaZulu player George Dearnaley recalls that it was common knowledge during his time that his team used muthi. 'It ranged from bathing in some prepared mixture, to having the kit "blessed", to having a muthi man in the dressing room, and also standing over a small fire burning with special leaves and sticks in the dressing room. We were also now and again given something to drink before a match, although none of the white guys ever swallowed the stuff. We put our lips to the cup, and then passed it on.'

'AmaZulu is a traditional club and it was not our place to criticise or judge the beliefs and cultural practice of the people running the club. As far as I was concerned, it was a case of "you do what you do, and I will do what I do" to get the best results,' he recalls.[13]

Dearnaley further tells of an AmaZulu match against Moroka Swallows at Ellis Park. The players were introduced to a 'muthi man' in the dressing room before the match. 'He wore a dark cloak and the dressing room was filled with candles. He stood in the middle of the players' circle and, for about five minutes, spoke very fast in Zulu. Next to me my teammate, Sazi Ngubane, was shaking with fear. Then the muthi man said, "From this night AmaZulu will *never* lose another match!"

'We were brilliant for the first ten minutes and when we scored, the muthi man ran across the field to the delight of the Usuthu[14] fans. We ended up losing 4–1 and never saw him again.'

In the second round match against Swallows in Durban a few months later, the regular team inyanga took him aside, he says, and gave him two small sticks. 'He said I must put one in each boot for luck. I thanked him, and as soon as I was out of his sight, threw them away. We won 4–1 and I scored two goals. I had forgotten about the sticks, until he jumped onto my back at the end of the game and promised me that for the next match he would give me three sticks!'

However, Dearnaley does give some credit to the psychological effect of muthi. 'I've seen the result muthi has on a player. It works on the guys who are more traditional in their beliefs. Simon 'CCV' Magagula once had a thigh injury that wouldn't heal. He went to physiotherapy and nothing worked. Eventually he went back to Middelburg to see his local muthi man who made a few small cuts in his leg and applied some herbs. Simon came back about two weeks later and was fit and ready to play.'

In a *Sunday Times* interview Frank 'Jingles' Pereira, who played with Stylianou at Chiefs, recalls the 'culture shocks' on joining the team, referring to the Friday night 'camping sessions' when rituals were conducted.[15] 'Our late masseur, Joe Mashinini, would gather the troops and shout, "Guys, come for a sauna!" The sauna was the primus stove with a pot full of boiling herbs. We had to cover ourselves with blankets and then steam.'

'When I told him I could not breathe, he said, "Hang in there my boy, the sauna will make you a better person." I never had a problem with the use of umuthi, but I did not want to be cut because it was against my religion,' referring to incisions made on players' bodies to 'give them strength'.

Surprisingly, many black players deny using muthi, even though most of them practice African rituals at home. This may be because of being sworn to secrecy during family rituals. Today, players moving between clubs to chase the best possible contracts comes at the expense of team loyalty. This has resulted in most of the rituals being done in secret, and only with trusted players or on outfits, so that the secrets of the club would not leak out if a player later joins a rival club. Drafting players from different clubs for the national squad also creates a major poser for a coach who wishes to employ rituals.

Soccer weekly *Soccer Laduma* carries a regular column on former players and often asks which of their teams used the most muthi. [16] All those interviewed now admit the prevailing use of muthi, and the clubs Pirates, Chiefs, Moroka Swallows and AmaZulu are often mentioned.

Ronnie Zondi, who played for Orlando Pirates, SuperSport United, Cape Town Spurs and Umtata Bush Bucks, says that of all the teams he played for, Pirates used muthi the most. Today he laughs about how they were made to chant '*iPirates ibone, iChiefs ingabone*' (let Pirates see, let Chiefs not see) as part of their ritual during his time at Pirates. He also recalls how his coach at Bush Bucks, Mlungisi Ngubane, made them inhale smoke from burning herbs.[17]

Under Jomo Sono as coach, Bafana Bafana were known to employ a person whose job description read 'Special Projects', although it was generally known that this was a muthi man. This clearly did not help the team, as the South African team did not perform particularly well at the time.

During the reign of Clive Barker, there was always a mystery man lurking among the technical team, who many believed to be a muthi man. 'Special Projects' team members often discreetly scatter muthi on the field to put a spell on their opponents. Sometimes a muthi man will request the name of a star player from the opposition, write it on a piece of paper and put it into a bottle containing a mixture of herbs and oils. This is done to ensure that the player does not perform well – a different take on 'bottling up' or 'containing' a player!

However, ahead of the 2002 Africa Cup of Nations tournament in Mali, the Confederation of African Football (CAF) banned 'team advisors' from being part of the official bench, saying it was a matter of image. In other words, they did not want the rest of the world to see African teams engaging in activities that could be construed as so-called Third World practices.

South Africa and the other African countries subsequently undertook not to use muthi men in their World Cup games in Korea and Japan later that year. One African commentator compared this decision to asking someone to go into an exam without a pen.

It is often argued that the activity is meant purely to psyche up players, and the 'Special Projects' team members play the same role as that of sports psychologists employed by Western sports teams and individual sport stars. Sportsmen often use visualisation, which in psychological terms entails creating a specific level of performance in your mind's eye before setting out to achieve that level. During visualisation, players go into a trance-like state, yet remain in total control. This phenomenon is also known as being in a 'flow'. It is reported that the legendary Pele was a practitioner of this method.

A visit to a witchdoctor apparently produces similar trance-like states. The inyanga or sangoma is sent into this state through drum beats and rhythmic chanting, singing and dancing, while the client is asked to visualise his objective – to win a game or to achieve something. The repeated chanting of 'siyavuma!' (we agree!) puts the player in a positive state of mind.

Essentially, the process is aimed at developing self-confidence through setting your own limits to allow performance at your full potential.

Superstition forms an undeniable part of soccer across the world. History records that in the early days, soccer teams did not change sides during half-time, and even in the so-called Western world, there were beliefs that one side of the field might be jinxed. It was only when the Federation of International Football Associations (FIFA) introduced the revised Cambridge Rules – the first set of uniform rules for the game – that changing of sides was made a part of the game.

In 2008 two players, one of them a star striker, were arrested in Oman in the United Arab Emirates for practicing 'black magic'. According to a news report, the players were arrested in Dubai along with two Omani 'sorcerers' because they had paid the Omanis to put a spell on national team selectors to ensure inclusion in the team.

The Dubai Sports Council, however, did not believe the arrests were part of a wider problem of 'black magic' in football in the region. 'This is a one-off incident and the practice isn't prevalent in UAE football. It's the players' personal choice to use black magic and very much their own decision,' Ahmed Mohammed al Rahomi, the council's spokesman, reportedly said. 'All that we know is that they were arrested for practising witchcraft.'[18]

Some Western coaches and players also have a few strange beliefs and employ a variety of techniques to ensure success. Former Italy coach, Giovanni Trapattoni, often sprinkled holy water on the playing field from a bottle provided by his sister, a nun. Some coaches and players believe certain colours are bad luck – Spanish coach Luis Aragonés reportedly believed that yellow is a bad sign, and once created quite a scene when a player arrived for a game wearing a yellow shirt. Spain lost the game. It is not known whether he insisted on his players keeping away from the colour in Euro 2008, which Spain won on a single strike against Germany.

England captain, John Terry, is said to believe in always sitting in the same seat on the bus when travelling to a game and always tying his shin pads up the same way – three times. If he does the same when playing for Chelsea, it clearly did not help him when his team met, and lost on penalties, to Manchester United in the European Club Champions league final in 2008: Terry missed a crucial penalty.

Does muthi really work? No one can really say, least of all me. What I do know is that for many South African coaches and players, maybe even the majority, the use of muthi and the services of a witchdoctor are an essential part of the game and they strongly believe in the effects. What some might see as clowning around between two soccer administrators that day in the *World*'s offices, others will take very seriously. Ewert Nene and Jimmy Sojane definitely believed strongly in anything – natural or supernatural – that would help them win a game. At the least, muthi is an interesting aspect of South Africa's soccer culture; at the most, it adds a kind of magic to the game.

2

Kick-off: The early years

For black South Africans, soccer is more than just 'the beautiful game'; it's the magic that lights up the dreary existence of township people, a sure ice-breaker between strangers. Match results, new player signings, refereeing decisions and predictions about the next game often form the pivot of early morning conversations at taxi ranks, on-the-job talk, mid-day breaks at the office and, of course, animated late night banter in shebeens.

Today, soccer has developed into the most popular team sport in South Africa. It draws some of the biggest crowds at sports events. Over 1.8 million players are registered and millions more play the game informally. Indeed, few blacks would have grown up without kicking a ball around in the dusty streets of the townships. The game has become a social and economic leveller, with many poor young boys escaping the poverty trap that the townships have become to enter a world of financial freedom they could not even have dreamt of.

Soccer stars instantly become heroes in their communities and are mimicked in street games, which are the hallmark of any township. The multimillion rand soccer industry has for many years been one of only two sectors – the other being the township taxi industry – where blacks were largely masters of their own destiny and could make fortunes as club owners.

Newspapers also cunningly use soccer's following to boost their profits. In all my years at the sports desk of newspapers such as *World*, *Post* and *Weekend World*, and later as editor of the *Sowetan*, weekly sales patterns were tied to soccer fixtures of the flanking weekends. Mondays were set aside for results and reviews of the past weekend's games; Tuesdays were to resolve outstanding arguments, including refereeing decisions, log positions and great escapes.

Come Wednesday, the build-up for the coming weekend's games would start. At the *World* we often tried to break a sports story on Wednesdays to boost flagging mid-week sales, with nothing better than the signing of a new player to create lively debate among readers. By Friday, interest in the coming weekend's games would have reached such a climax that soccer would almost be the sole subject of discussion on buses, trains and taxis. And by Monday the cycle would start anew.

At its height, *World* was the biggest selling daily newspaper in the country – thanks to its robust focus on soccer. To reporters on the *World* there were only two important addresses in Johannesburg: 11 Newclare Road, Industria (the address of the newspaper) and Number 11, Orlando East, opposite Orlando Stadium.

The latter was always the centre of soccer talk and one of the favourite haunts for our soccer reporters. Naturally, it was a 'Pirates house' and the arguments about who to field and who not to field on match day would start early afternoon over copious amounts of beer, grog and *mahog* – spirit alcohol and brandy respectively – before fans rushed into the stadium across the road to book their seats. When the informants' tongues had been adequately loosed by over-consumption, many a story about teams and players could be picked up there . . .

For all its present following, the game of soccer has a long history, not only in South Africa but also elsewhere in the world. Official soccer records date the beginning of the game to a misty day in England in December 1863. Participants in a totally uncontrolled game, which had built up a reputation for riotous behaviour, shin kicking, tripping and carrying the ball, decided the time had come to clean up the game and formally codify their pastime. With one group in favour of a game where ball handling was allowed and the other against, rugby and football developed into two separate sports. Following two months of debate over the rules that should govern the new game among the football group – mostly alumni from public schools and universities where the game had taken root – the way was paved for the formation of the Football Association of England.

Records indicate that soccer games were first played in China in the second and third centuries BC.[19] A military manual dating from the Han Dynasty describes an exercise where a leather ball filled with feathers and hair had to be kicked through a 30–40-cm-wide opening into a small net held up by bamboo canes. In another version, a player would be obstructed in his 'goal-scoring' attempt and had to use his feet, chest and shoulders to clear his way for shooting.

Other forms of the game also existed in the Far East and in ancient Greece, while the Roman version featured two teams playing on a marked field, each passing the ball around their opponents in an attempt to get it over the boundary lines of the opposition. It is even said that the severed head of a Danish prince once served as a 'ball', but this story is most likely apocryphal.

After centuries of unruly ball kicking, the game has evolved from one where 'any means could be employed to score, with the exception of murder and manslaughter' to today's soccer governed by FIFA Fairplay rules, where a tackle with intent to injure your opponent is punished and players are even sent off for repeat offences. [20]

As South Africa was a British colony in the nineteenth century, it is not surprising that soccer was soon being played here. Many of the early soccer matches in South Africa featured British civil servants and soldiers posted to the colony – 'fifteen officers of the army' playing against 'a like number of gentlemen in the civil service'.[21] British troops deployed to war territories during the respective wars against the Zulus and Boers in the late nineteenth century were keenly watched by locals when they played soccer during quiet moments.

Although the first soccer games in South Africa were reputedly played along the Cape coast – in Cape Town and Port Elizabeth around 1862 – the province then called Natal can be regarded as the birthplace of organised soccer in South Africa. It is believed that the first properly constituted club in South Africa was a team known as Pietermaritzburg County, founded in 1879 by a group of white settlers. Indian and African clubs were active in both Durban and Johannesburg by 1880, but the white Natal clubs were the first to form an official soccer association in the country, namely the whites-only Natal Football Association established in 1882.[22] Indian clubs formed the Transvaal Indian Football Association in 1896.

Indian and African service workers on the Durban docks had established four soccer teams by 1886. Natal soccer has since had a long and proud history, with a team such as Bush Bucks FC (formed in Durban in 1902) featuring in the top ranks of South African soccer for almost a hundred years since its establishment.

By 1910 Durban had become something of a major soccer centre for Africans, with as many as seven African teams. Most of these teams had what was perceived to be an elitist foundation, made up of educated and employed workers. But African Wanderers, however, was the first 'people's team', accepting players from all ranks and social standing in communities.

The team was founded in Pietermaritzburg,[23] but later also included members from Ladysmith and Newcastle. This resulted in tough competition for playing spots, and as a consequence several splits occurred in the team as players sought ways to ensure they played regularly. Some of the teams that were born from this are Ladysmith Home Boys and Newcastle Home Lads. Another split in 1939 led to the formation of the Zulu Royals, which is today known as AmaZulu following various disputes over the name.[24]

American missionaries greatly contributed to popularising and developing soccer in Natal through establishing teams such as Ocean Swallows in Umbumbulu, Natal Cannons in Inanda, and Adams College Shooting Stars from Amanzimtoti.

The Amanzimtoti Training Institute, later known as Adams College, and its soccer team, Shooting Stars, deserve special mention. The college was founded by the American Board of Commissioners for Foreign Missions and was considered among the best public missionary schools for blacks in the country. Stars were to become one of the most respected and technically astute teams in Durban, and as the most prestigious team in the region, every boy wanted to play for them.

They also began playing outside of the college environment and against other teams in the region. By 1908 they had established themselves as champions. The major advantage that Stars had over other teams was that the college had its own, albeit limited, facilities and did not depend on the municipality-controlled grounds. This meant that the team could train when they wanted to and were largely independent from any government control. But the only way to play for Stars was to become a student at the college, which, of course, helped the enrolment at Adams College no end.

Albert Luthuli, Nobel laureate and former president of the African National Congress (ANC), was probably one of the most influential people associated with Adams College, where he studied and taught for several years. Apart from becoming a prominent leader in the struggle against apartheid, he also played a major role in the development of soccer in South Africa.

After the death of his father, the ten-year-old Albert, who had been living in the former Rhodesia (Zimbabwe), returned to a village on the northern Natal coast where he learned Zulu traditions and duties in the household of his uncle, the chief of Groutville.

Educated through his mother's earnings as a washerwoman and supplemented by a scholarship, the young Luthuli enrolled at Ohlange Institute, a school founded by Dr John Dube, who was also its principal at the time. Ohlange was a black college based on the Tuskeegee Institute in Atlanta in the United States of America.

Luthuli left Ohlange to train as a teacher at Edendale Methodist School outside Pietermaritzburg. Shortly after qualifying as a teacher, he enrolled at Adams College for a secondary school teacher training course on a government scholarship. He declined a scholarship for further study at Fort Hare in order to work and support his ailing mother, and took up a teaching position at Adams College.

Luthuli was a serious proponent of the principle that a healthy body houses a healthy mind, a view shaped by his Methodist education. Soccer, he believed, supported the ideas of the social drive of the twenties to moralise the leisure time of black South Africans.

'Games develop and call for the exercise of those qualities

which contribute to the highest manhood, and for most of us they help to keep us occupied in our leisure moments when otherwise the devil would be finding work for our idle hands,' Luthuli argued.[25]

Adams College hosted several games and became a hub of social and sporting life in Durban. Despite life at Adams being somewhat insulated from what was happening in South Africa,[26] Luthuli recognised the potential of soccer to create greater political awareness among fans and players. He was the first secretary of the (black) South African African Football Association (SAAFA) and was instrumental in transforming sport administration towards non-racialism through the formation of the Natal Inter-Race Soccer Board with Rev. Bernard Sigamoney.

The board managed to arrange a few games and is generally accepted as the forerunner to the first soccer body committed to non-racialism, the South African Soccer Federation (SASF), which was founded in 1951. Its objective was to challenge the racial divisions within soccer by arranging games between Africans, Indians and Coloureds. Luthuli believed the game transcended cultural and race lines, and saw the value for political mobilisation.

Luthuli also observed that soccer afforded him the opportunity to interact with all kinds of people. 'I think what has attracted me as much as the game has been the opportunity to meet all sorts of people, from the loftiest to the most disreputable,' he wrote.[27]

'I became a compulsive football fan. To this day, I am carried away helplessly by the excitement of a soccer match . . . '[28]

The idea that sport can unite people from different backgrounds still holds. At a seminar a few years ago Deputy President Kgalema Motlanthe, then Secretary General of the ANC, described sport as networks of associations among the poor and the working class that build solidarity to respond to specific challenges that affect them.[29] 'Such challenges include eradicating poverty, advancing the moral well-being of the community, the quest for better sports facilities, combating crime, campaigning for better transport, and working to improve the health and education of members of the community,' he said.

As an example of sport inspiring community mobilisation, Motlanthe cited the example of resistance by the community of Mangaung in Bloemfontein in the sixties. Being denied the use of council sports grounds after the local soccer association refused to be co-opted by the government-supported South African Bantu Football Association (SABFA), the community resorted to playing on an open field that was cleared and levelled. Every Friday the council would send in bulldozers to dig up the pitch; every Saturday morning the community would turn up to level the field in time for the afternoon's games.

Following years of negotiations between missionaries, officials from the black clubs and the superintendent of the Municipal Depot (Somtseu Road) Men's Hostel, the Durban and District Native Football Association (DDNFA) was finally formed in 1916. In accordance with changing political sentiments, it later changed its name to the Durban and District African Football Association (DDAFA). Formalising soccer firmly established the game in the province and resulted in keen inter-town competition, featuring teams from Durban, Ladysmith, Newcastle and later also Pietermartizburg.

Durban was fast becoming the key port for the goods from the Witwatersrand. As migrant workers left the rural areas to settle in the city, Durban experienced substantial population growth during the first half of the nineteenth century. This steady migration led to the city's municipality devising ways, such as implementing the Natal Native Locations Act of 1904 that forced the black population to live in certain areas, to control the worker influx. A night curfew was also introduced to ensure blacks retired to their residences in the black townships before nightfall.

As urbanisation increased, soccer grew from an elitist game to one in which ordinary workers participated, and one supported by ordinary people. However, drunkenness often marred the games. Drinking was blamed for activities such as gambling at informal soccer games, which invariably led to conflicts and often mayhem. The Natal Parliament passed the Native Beer Act of 1908, which outlawed the home brewing of African beer and only allowed the drink to be sold (and consumed) at designated beer halls. The purpose of the law was to raise revenue for the Native Beer Administration Fund, ostensibly to build new locations, schools, hospitals and other facilities and additional hostels for migrant workers, but was in reality used more to finance the Native Administration offices in Durban and Pietermaritzburg. Although also meant to control the unruly fans who consumed beer in uncontrolled circumstances, most of the beer halls were built close to the soccer grounds, thereby increasing the very risk controlled drinking was meant to manage.

Government officials soon realised that soccer could be used as a way to control the black population by keeping them entertained and so distracting them from their woeful socio-economic fate. The same sentiment was later echoed by The Chamber of Mines newspaper, *Umteteli wa Bantu,* which stated in a report that various sports had been organised for mine workers on the Rand's gold fields 'and in various other ways, provision is made to keep the natives wholesomely amused.'[30] Rudimentary soccer fields were provided to 'keep the natives busy during their leisure time'.[31] The need for social control over the 'natives' was a particular concern among white officials for many years.

Soccer as a form of social control became the norm against the spectre of unemployment, crime and the growth of political awareness as urbanisation surged. In the years that followed, the desire to control was always supreme in the minds of the white bureaucrats put in charge of 'native affairs'. In the 1930s, for example, the Native Welfare Officer of the Durban municipality demanded that his permission be sought if teams wanted to charge fans for admission to their games. The municipality provided only £1,000–1,500 annually for 'native' sport and recreation, half of which went to the salary of the Welfare Officer.[32]

Not satisfied with this arrangement, the Council went even further to ensure the DDAFA did not become self-sufficient. They established what was known as the Bantu Recreational Grounds Association, which demanded an additional 15% cut from all gate takings by the DDAFA.[33]

While the white associations were given massive funding towards the building of the new Kingsmead ground in Durban, as well as the Durban Council making funds available for rugby and cricket facilities in their 1957–8 appropriation, the black soccer associations in Natal had to raise whatever funds they needed themselves.[34]

Limited funds were provided for renovations to the Somtseu Road grounds – five grass fields, eight ticket offices, eleven turnstiles, a fence and a brick wall to enclose the stadium – on the fringe of downtown Durban by the mid-1950s.

But this was hardly benevolence on the part of the Council. Indian–African riots in 1949 resulted in 142 people being killed, more than a thousand injured and many Indian-owned buildings and shops being destroyed. The brick wall surrounding the stadium was, in reality, meant to keep blacks away from the adjoining municipal barracks for Indian workers as the Council feared a flare-up of friction. It also reinforced the government's principle of separate development.

Despite limited Council funds, the DDAFA was reputedly the richest sporting organisation in Natal by 1950. In 1959 it was able to buy land to the value of £7,800 on a mission reserve to create playing fields.[35] Henry Ngwenya, President of the DDAFA and SAAFA in the 1950s, argued that soccer had an entrepreneurial appeal and often provided blacks the only legal means of accumulating wealth.[36]

Today there are many black players and administrators who turned their involvement in soccer into a profitable pastime – Irvin Khoza, technically the owner of Orlando Pirates, is top of the list. His wealth enabled him to bankroll the national soccer association to the tune of R4 million a few years ago. Then there is Kaizer Motaung, founder of Kaizer Chiefs, Jabu Phakathi of AmaZulu, Mato Madlala of Lamontville Golden Arrows, the late David Chabeli of Moroka Swallows, Ria Ledwaba, former owner of Ria Stars, and Mike Mokoena (Free State Stars). Jomo Sono, who has a vast portfolio of business interests, also has soccer to thank for his fortune.

Natal was also at the forefront of developing black soccer on a national level. By 1932 negotiations between the Transvaal African Football Association and its Natal counterpart, the DDAFA led by T Ngcobo and Albert Luthuli, had resulted in the formation of SAAFA, who strove for greater independence of black soccer associations. The Orange Free State association joined the national association in 1934, followed by the Cape Board in 1936.

The word 'African' in SAAFA's name reflects a particular political position which emphasised a commitment by the organisation to become self-sufficient and not be co-opted by structures created or supported by the government of the day. It stood in direct opposition to SABFA, which was established in 1933 and received financial and other support from the government – an effort the government had hoped would stem the tide of anti-establishment feeling that was simmering at the time.

SAAFA decided to take the game to the next level by seeking sponsorship for an interprovincial tournament. Officials approached AF Baumann of Bakers Limited, a Durban biscuit company, and with its sponsorship SAAFA launched the first major organised soccer tournament, known as the Bakers Cup.

Natal hosted, and won, the first edition of the tournament in August 1932 at the hot and humid Somtseu Road grounds, and retained the title the following year at the Bantu Sports Ground in Johannesburg. The Cape did not send a representative team due to the prohibitive cost of sending up a team.[37]

The fierce competition in soccer resulted in referees often being attacked. Again Natal led the way when, in 1932, soccer referees formed a union to protect themselves from attacks – the first association of its kind in the country.

In 1953 the DDAFA featured in the Centenary Soccer Tournament in Southern Rhodesia, which they won. Natal blazed the trail once more by appointing British coach Topper Brown to manage a representative team of the province. They were the first province to appoint a white full-time coach and in 1955, Brown led the Natal Africans to victory in both the Moroka–Baloyi Cup and the Natal Inter-Race Singh Cup.

Durban teams also performed extremely well in the South African Soccer League (SASL) in the sixties. When the league was eventually strangled to death by officialdom through denied use of facilities, the SASF took advantage of the expulsion of Coloured and Indian players from black African teams and formed a six-team professional league, with the former Durban-based SASL teams forming the backbone. But again, the league could not raise adequate sponsorship and was doomed to failure.

Despite the influential position of Natal teams on the early South African soccer scene, the glory days have yet to return to the province. Teams such as Durban Bush Bucks, Lamontville Golden Arrows, Zulu Royals (AmaZulu), Manning Rangers, Maritzburg United and Durban African Wanderers experienced mixed success at national premier league level, often failing to maintain consistent positions. In the 1996–7 season, Manning Rangers gave the province the honour of winning the first Premiership title, but was relegated to the lower league in 2005 and eventually went bankrupt in 2006. The club was later bought by the financial services group Fidentia, but has since perished following the collapse of Fidentia. After just one year in the Premiership, Maritzburg United was relegated to the National First Division in 2006. However, having won the National First Division championship in 2007–8, it rejoined Ama-Zulu, Thanda Royal Zulu and Golden Arrows to represent KwaZulu-Natal in the elite league. At the end of the 2008–9 season, Thanda was relegated, leaving only Arrows, AmaZulu and Maritzburg in the Premier league.

Just as the promise of opportunity and wealth led to the rise of Natal soccer, so it probably also signalled the end of its reign. Through the years the glitter of gold has lured many talented Natal players to the vibrant life on the Reef. The trend continues today, as the bustling economic activity of Gauteng offers players a better chance at soccer fame and fortune.

3

The battle for access to fields

Many Natal players were enchanted by the City of Gold. The Johannesburg they experienced during short team tours seemed to glisten with opportunity. Yet those who moved inland soon found all that glitters is not necessarily gold. Life on the Reef was harsh, uncompromising, tough.

Working Johannesburg was a drab city of comings and goings, of sweaty humanity. On the mines, black men were confined to single-sex hostels that were divided according to ethnic groups. These single sex-hostels were meant not only as accommodation but also as, according to sociologist Lawrence Schlemmer's description, 'social enclaves' with a 'different political culture and different kinds of interest than [for] the surrounding township dwellers'.[38]

The loneliness of a hostel dweller can hardly be described. Music provided some escape and the sounds of *isicatamiya* – traditional Zulu music – often filled the air. Sitting in the morning sun on those rare weekend days when they had a break, or when they were on the afternoon shift, some workers would twang their guitars or play concertinas while wailingly, pleadingly almost, singing '*Unzima lomhlaba*' (It's a tough world) – the longing for home undeniable.

Others would seek refuge from the chaos and penury in the

readily available Bantu beer (an alcoholic drink made from sorghum), or comfort from the ever-present women who hung around the hostels and offered their services for a fee. Still others would engage in tribal contests of song and dance, and at other times they would even get into fisticuffs, creating groups called *amalaita* (bare-knuckle fighters). But more often workers would escape to the soccer grounds – perhaps their biggest indulgence.

Miriam Makeba lamented the deaths of black workers on the mines in one of her famous protest songs *Gauteng*; Hugh Masekela protested the notorious train that brought the migrant mine workers from all over Southern Africa to feed the labour needs of the mining houses, and to be dispensed with when either ill or dead, knowing the supply chain would continue to provide cheap labour for industries and mine houses.

Beyond the hostels, black urbanisation led to acute housing shortages in Johannesburg, accompanied by unemployment and increased crime levels.

In 1920 the townships were created as 'native locations' to accommodate migrants. The Native Administration Act of 1927 gave the Governor General the power to rule by proclamation, and he could remove any African group or person from one location to another anywhere in South Africa – an instrument that township superintendents used quite ruthlessly to get rid of people they decided were, for whatever reason, undesirable.

Growing political militancy caused much concern among both government and the Chamber of Mines, who began to see sport promotion as a possible lever for social control. Fears that unemployment gave blacks more time in which to reflect upon their oppressed situation encouraged mining houses to expand recreational facilities. The move was probably a gilt-edged investment – at the same time providing entertainment for blacks and diverting attention from political influences.

When soccer was first organised in South Africa, officials in charge of 'native affairs' and the missionaries involved with the game believed that organised sport would teach Africans a 'new conformity and instil social discipline through play', and saw unorganised initiatives as both an impediment to African 'racial progress' and an obstacle to compliant urban assimilation.[39] Soccer associations were also established in order to reduce the number of informal games and 'to rid [the game of] gambling' and 'other objectionable practices' that were associated with such games.[40]

For the white officials, soccer provided a manner of social control and the mining houses, which employed the majority of black Africans who had arrived on the Reef to provide labour to the burgeoning mining sector, supported this view. Surprisingly, however, the facilities that were provided for black soccer players – and black sport in general – did not match the level of concern and objective of social control. This was mostly as a result of the underpinning philosophy that blacks were temporary sojourners in 'white' South Africa, and would, in due course, return to their rural homelands.

It was against this backdrop that black soccer's struggle for acknowledgement played out. One way in which government and mining houses tried to appease blacks was by creating 'native' or 'Bantu' soccer structures. With the closure of the mine-based league by the late twenties, mine clerks, with the support of a group of white philanthropists, established the Johannesburg Bantu Football Association (JBFA). The JBFA kicked off with 20 teams of the approximately 45 that existed in the City of Gold at the time.

At its inception two white men – American Board missionary

Rev. Ray Phillips and the manager of the Non-European Affairs Department (NEAD), Graham Ballenden – were at the helm of the JBFA: Phillips as vice-president and Ballenden as 'patron'. In addition, the association also had as 'honorary presidents' other white men – AW Oliver, who was superintendent of the townships of Orlando and Klipspruit, and LA Venables, a deputy manager in the NEAD.

It soon became clear that the white administrators of Bantu organisations would thrust black officials to the front, while they still pulled the strings in the background. One such official was Sol Senaoane, the first black sports organiser for the NEAD, who was also involved in the founding of the JBFA. By involving officials such as Senaoane, the NEAD strengthened its hold on the soccer association. As such the black press often referred to the JBFA as having been 'municipalised', which was later said to have been born and bred in the Non-European Affairs Department.

Another structure created by white liberals was the Bantu Men's Social Centre (BMSC). It was set up in a building next to the performance venue Dorkay House on the southern fringe of the Johannesburg city centre. Founded in 1924 by Phillips and another American Board missionary, Frederick Bridgeman, the centre was run and controlled by a white administration.

'Healthy, uplifting recreation is the key to winning over the raw native,' Bridgeman averred. The BMSC's main objective was 'to get natives under wholesome influences during their spare time and counteract the tendency for them to stroll about the streets on Saturdays and Sundays when they fall into temptation through the influence of agitators.'[41]

The BMSC soon became a hub of social and political activity among black city dwellers. The ANC Youth League was founded at this venue in 1944 and the wedding reception of ANC stalwarts Walter Sisulu and Albertina Metetiwe took place there, attended by, among others, Nelson Mandela and Anton Lembede. The farewell function for Father Trevor Huddleston was also held at the BMSC in 1956.

The first superintendent of the BMSC was Richard V Selope-Thema, who held the position until 1932 when he left to take up a position as editor of the *Bantu World*. But when the trustees had difficulty finding a white member to fill a key administrative position, a black African, JR Rathebe, was appointed amidst much debate and opposition from some members. The fact that he was a school teacher of seventeen years' standing, five of which as a principal, counted for little in the view of those who opposed the appointment of a black person.

In 1931 the Bantu Sports Club (BSC) was established on former mining ground on the outskirts of Johannesburg to complement the BMSC. Once again Rev. Phillips was involved. There was enough space for a soccer field, tennis courts, a clubhouse and stands for about 5,000 spectators. The club was one of the few unrestricted facilities for blacks and was more than just a sports club.[42] It also hosted parties, socials, dance competitions and rallies.

At its peak, it had over 1,000 members, with soccer crowd attendance reaching 12,000 for some games.[43] It also had a small library, and ran a night school. Originally, the club was run by trustees, missionaries, government officials and representatives from the Chamber of Mines, while blacks were accommodated in sub-committees.

The JBFA and the Johannesburg African Football Association (JAFA) both affiliated to the club to allow their member teams access to facilities and so shared in the admission revenue.

In 1934 a set of trustees was appointed to regulate the allocation of the BSC's grounds and facilities among the two associations (the JBFA and JAFA). Soccer administrator Dan Twala, who was also one of the founders of JAFA, was appointed to manage the facilities – a position initially held by a white.

JAFA, which by 1943 had over 1,200 players, ran a 'well-organised competition' at the BSC, and had attendances of 'up to 10,000 spectators at their Sunday games'.[44]

When the BSC decided to reduce entrance fees to attract more people to the games without consulting the two associations, it caused such tension that the JBFA eventually withdrew from the club. Their matches were moved to the nearby Wemmer Sports Grounds – a facility run by the NEAD.

JAFA declared that it would remain independent of white control. The so-called 'Bantu' associations were widely regarded as 'sweetheart' organisations of the municipality and this prompted a move towards 'Africanisation' by many organisations fighting for true independence. JAFA went on to form their own provincial association, the Transvaal African Football Association (TAFA), which described itself as an association by Africans for Africans.

This action angered the white officials, including the board members of the trust controlling the BSC, who accused JAFA of lack of cooperation.

Not surprisingly, the white administrators decided to limit their funding to the BSC, prompting Twala to seek additional funding from other sources. These efforts largely failed. With such limited funding, Twala struggled to keep the club afloat and attempts at encouraging employers to pay for the subscriptions of their black employees did not attract much response either. Determined, Twala laboured on and turned his attention to getting support from black Africans themselves. He appealed to transport authorities to ensure adequate transport for the domestic workers from the northern suburbs to attend events at the BSC in the south, but again without much success.

The trustees threatened to sell part of the land and assets of the club or to hand the land over to the Johannesburg Council, which, if this were to happen, would put JAFA right back under the control of whites – a situation from which they thought they had extricated themselves when they affiliated to the BSC.

For years, Twala worked hard to remain independent from the municipality. His political, social and cultural consciousness grew, and soon the BSC facilities were used for more than just sport. Both political meetings and trade union rallies were held there, among them a May Day demonstration for recognition of African trade unions and demonstrations for the abolition of pass laws. In 1944 the ANC sponsored a soccer tournament at the BSC.

Twala described the club as the national home of all tribal activities; the arena for national events like the Mendi Memorial Service (commemorating the sinking of the SS *Mendi* during World War II, with 647 troops – 607 of them black South Africans – aboard) and the Assemblies of Zulus and Swazis. It was the venue for many pageants, demonstrations, exhibitions and inter-provincial tournaments.

The financial squeeze kept tightening and with the club simply not generating enough revenue to keep it going, the end was inevitable. Other factors conspired to hasten the demise of the BSC. Twala had complained about illicit liquor sales in a strip between the beer hall and the club facilities, but the NEAD failed to respond to the complaint. Even the Mining Commissioner estimated that 27,000 Africans gathered at the beer hall and soccer grounds. He warned that the military would have to intervene should a fight or unrest break out. The police urged the municipality to close down both the sports ground and the beer hall.[45]

But it was the municipality that had built the beer hall opposite the BSC, ostensibly to control and manage drinking ahead of and after soccer matches, but, if the truth be told, to take marketing advantage of the thousands of blacks who gathered there. The municipality eventually bought the troublesome strip of land and fenced it into the BSC, using corrugated iron fencing. Access to the ground, through only a single entrance, was under NEAD police supervision.

Financial difficulties, together with the discomfort and displeasure of the liberal trustees over usage of the club facilities, eventually sounded the death knell for the club in 1948. The NEAD bought the BSC for £150,000, but undertook that the facilities would continue to be used for the benefit of the black community. It claimed success in turning the BSC into a first class sports stadium for blacks – in reality a misnomer for the poorly maintained facility – and renamed it the Bantu Sports Ground, as opposed to club, in order to narrow the activities that could take place there.

When the Johannesburg City Council took control of the BSC through the NEAD, JAFA insisted on a legal lease clause to ensure that they did not get kicked off the only grounds at their disposal. At that point the Council had denied them access to other facilities under its control. The NEAD accepted the clause, with the proviso that they would share the gate-takings from the games under JAFA. Not only that: 30% of gross takings during matches featuring representative teams would go to the NEAD, while all costs had to be borne by JAFA. Lastly, they could only use the grounds for six months every year, which meant clubs would remain idle for the remaing period as they did not have access to other facilities.

These additional conditions were unacceptable to JAFA, but when they voiced their concern, the NEAD simply suggested that the same conditions would be offered to the JBFA, who would, no doubt, be willing to accept them. That would have been the death knell for JAFA and so they reluctantly accepted the conditions – and thus to be firmly under the financial control of the NEAD.

To further increase the misery of JAFA, the BSC clubhouse burnt down under extremely suspicious circumstances, and JAFA's records were lost in the fire. The NEAD continued to deny JAFA the use of other municipal soccer grounds, as they insisted that they did not recognise the association – although happily taking the 30% of their gate-takings from games at the BSC.

In 1950 JAFA faced a major test of principle when a friendly series was arranged in Katanga Province in the then Belgian Congo, jointly organised by the South African embassy and the NEAD. The idea was to select a team of players from both the African and the Bantu associations, which would have been led and managed by a white official – presumably to ensure that the black players were not exposed to a culture different from that which they were used to, although the South African consul had assured his bosses that there was no 'fraternisation between Europeans and Natives in Congo'.[46]

The African association rejected this offer, largely because the players had to pay for themselves, and because they refused to have a white official lead the team. They were also suspicious of the political intentions of the NEAD. The Bantu group, however, accepted the invitation. The Johannesburg team was thrashed 8–0 in the final of the tournament.

Black soccer's struggle for independence continued into the 1950s. It also played out in already existing national football structures, which were based on the prejudices and the racial template decreed by the white government. Each racial group formed its own teams and separate national associations, not including players or members from other racial groups. The (white) South African Football Association (SAFA) had been the first to be established (1892) and was later renamed the Football Association of South Africa (FASA). The South African Indian Football Association was established in 1903, followed by SABFA in 1933 and the South African Coloured Football Association in 1936, while the African organisation, SAAFA, was formed in 1932.

The NEAD afforded soccer organisations that carried the 'Bantu' name sole access to all municipality-controlled sports grounds. By the late 1950s SABFA was one of the main role players and firmly established under the rule of its imposing president, Bethuel Morolo. He would dominate the black soccer scene for nearly two decades.

Morolo was an enigma. Publicly, he would declare his opposition to apartheid, but insist that he could work only within what was legally possible within structures established by the government. However, he seemed to have been easily swayed by NEAD and other government officials, who would dangle largesse to make him come around to their point of view. His association being in control of the best facilities put him at a great advantage over the African and non-racial associations. But in most cases, his undoing was the poor administrative capability at his disposal – mostly men appointed because they would not dare oppose him.

The policies he pursued put him in direct conflict with those struggling for non-racial sport in South Africa. As a result, he was often accused of being in cahoots with the white establishment and a stooge of the apartheid government.

In reality, however, he took on all opponents – including the white soccer establishment. He challenged the white-governed FASA several times and communicated directly with FIFA to make his own case for recognition. On the other hand, he also grounded several attempts to launch a black professional league that was not on his terms. His actions can be compared to those of the homeland leaders of later years.

He was articulate, and often told me during our daily one-hour train commute between Pretoria and Johannesburg that, although he did not have much of a formal education, he had a deep hunger for knowledge and the intelligence to digest it. 'I read,' he would declare. And this showed, as he could quote liberally from the great English literatures. This often put him at an advantage over delegates to SABFA meetings, some of whom were barely literate.

His gaunt look often led his opponents to mistakenly believe that they could take him on in argument or intellectual discourse; many left bruised. His bristling presence was enough to inspire and intimidate. Even those who disagreed with him – and there were several – would nod in agreement and express support for his policies when in his presence.

Morolo was an astute administrator and a stickler for constitutional procedures. His knowledge of the constitutions of the various associations – including his own – was often used with devastating effect at meetings. He always carried a briefcase, which contained, among others, the statutes of FIFA and a host of other soccer-related documents. In any discussion, he would open the briefcase, and produce a document to support his arguments.

But the one most important to him was the constitution of SABFA. His knowledge of the association's constitution was so extensive that he was called 'Mr Constitution'. Several meetings were in fact abandoned because he had proven them to be unconstitutional.

When he was honoured at the fiftieth anniversary celebrations of CAF in 2007, it almost seemed a contradiction to list Morolo and white administrators Viv Granger, Dave Snaier and Fred Fell along with Ashwin Trikamjee, Norman Middleton, Rama Reddy, Dan Twala and Danny Jordaan, who fought so relentlessly against the apartheid system.

Morolo's leadership of SABFA often caused conflict, not only with the white-governed FASA but later also among his own constituency. By 1969 SABFA executives Joe Sibiya, George Thabe and PJ Maupa had launched a major drive, dubbed 'Morolo must go', to remove him from office.

Various strategies for his overthrow were crafted in the smoke-filled meeting rooms of Kim's Rest Inn in Katlehong, east of Johannesburg – one of the few meeting venues available to blacks. During several such meetings officials from provincial associations would put forward a motion for a special SABFA executive meeting, where a new president could be elected. Sibiya, then president of the Transvaal Bantu Football Association (TBFA), was suggested as a suitable candidate to replace Morolo, but fell short when it came to implementation. Failing to mobilise committed support from the provincial associations to remove Morolo, Sibiya was eventually voted out of office and replaced by George Thabe.

The meetings were held on Sundays and were always open to the press. Invariably I was the only journalist to attend, as the only other black newspaper was the Sunday paper *Post*. The role of the media in supporting the campaign was significant. Ahead of these special SABFA executive meetings, headlines in the *World* would scream the demise of Morolo as president. On the train, Morolo often waved the paper in my face, confidently declaring that we would run another 'Morolo still president' headline on the Monday following the meeting. 'Those who think they can easily get rid of me can forget about it – I have enough support to survive any attempt by the minority who wish to oust me,' he told me, to laughter from other passengers. For several years, this was indeed the case.

Morolo was master of everything related to black soccer for decades. But in the end he knew he could not hold on forever. He knew that the knives were out and would be plunged into his back at the first opportunity. And, being the astute administrator that he was, he could read the signs that his adversaries would eventually muster enough support to oust him. South African soccer continued to flounder in this turmoil, as the focus was on administration rather than on getting a professional league off the ground. Sponsors who had tried to keep black soccer afloat were retreating following several failed attempts to form and run a professional league. It became clear that only a change in management could save the game.

Early in 1970 George Thabe challenged Morolo to call a special general meeting during which an executive would be elected to run SABFA. Thabe was then president of the TBFA and treasurer of SABFA. During the 1971 biennial meeting of SABFA, Morolo knew that his reign was about to end. Rather than face the prospect of losing an election battle, he walked out of the meeting, declaring it unconstitutional. This time, however, he had little support or sympathy. George Thabe was finally elected to replace Morolo and a long, controversial career came to an end. Thereafter Morolo disappeared from the soccer scene and he died quietly at his home in Atteridgeville, Pretoria, in 2003.

The end of Morolo's rule concluded an era fraught with internal struggle among the black soccer community. Yet, at the height of apartheid and with pressure from the international sporting community mounting, more was to come.

4

What's in a name?

Soccer supporters across the world go to the extreme to support
their favourite teams and players. Face painting and dressing
up in the finest regalia depicting your team is found around
the world – South African fans even paint their houses in the
colours of their beloved teams!

Kaizer Chiefs fans, proudly displaying the team logo and
colours, declare to be 'Khosi for life',[47] while Orlando Pirates
fans – 'The Ghost'– commit themselves as 'Once a Pirate, always
a Pirate'. Bloemfontein Celtic fans again call themselves 'Siwelele
sa Masokolara' (gathering of the nightriders) and Moroka Swallows fans advise 'don't follow me, follow the Birds'. Supporters
of Mamelodi Sundowns believe that 'The sky is the limit', and
proudly call their team 'Bafana ba Style' (the boys with style).

Local fans feel so passionately about the game and its players
that disputes over soccer matters have driven families apart.
In a few instances such disputes have even led to assaults and
death.

Another uniquely South African aspect to the game is the
names teams choose for themselves. Apart from some fascinating and strange team names – Fight-For-Evers, Try Again and
London Walk Away FC spring to mind – the majority of South
African teams prefer their names to reflect something of local

relevance. References to animals or cultural heritage have often featured, for example, Ocean Swallows, Bush Bucks, Ohlange Wild Zebras, Wemmer Blue Birds, Hungry Lions, Vultures, Cape Ramblers and Black Hunters, to name a few.

The names of several English Football Association teams who have toured South Africa before the sport boycott in the 1960s have also stuck: teams such as Arsenal, Liverpool, Hotspur, Rangers, Manchester and even Preston Brothers – presumably coined from Preston North End – are found in the amateur ranks. There are also others, like Blackpool, Kliptown Burnley, Orlando Highlanders and Avalon Athletic that reflect the British influence.

Even some English mottos can be heard, albeit with a South African twist: the Bloemfontein Celtic fans' maxim '*Kae kapa ka, ke tla tsamaya le wena*' (wherever you go, I will walk with you) reminds us of the Liverpool FC anthem *You'll never walk alone* (used also as a motto by Umtata Bucks).

When you consider the important contribution of soccer during the struggle against political oppression, it is not surprising that some team names had political undertones. Brothers Aziz and Essop Pahad, both involved in the struggle for liberation and later deputy minister and minister respectively in the ANC government, were instrumental in the formation of a Johannesburg team called Dynamos. The reference to the Ukranian team Dynamo Kiev, then playing in the Soviet Union, was a subtle link to the communist influence that cunningly escaped the security police. Another team with a masked political connotation to their name was Lenasia Swaraj from the Johannesburg township Lenasia, which was designated for Indians. Swaraj referred to a political party that fought for self-government and opposed British rule in India. Also, the Orlando Pirates saying '*Ezimnyama ngenkani*' (black whether you like it or not) was

a show of assertiveness in the face of social pressures and oppression. It might even have been an early manifestation of the
Black Power philosophy. Indeed, Salthiel Chochoe, former Bucs
defender and proponent of black consciousness, was often
greeted with shouts of 'Black Power!'

Financial pressures have forced many teams to attach the
name of a sponsor to their own, often at the expense of the as-
piration to reflect a unique and individual character in their
names. For example, Arcadia Shepherds have changed their
name to Arcadia Pepsi, became Arcadia Fluoride when that
sponsorship terminated, and then later reverted to their original name; Mpumalanga Black Aces has cycled through Witbank
Black Aces, Ukhamba Black Aces, Super Curl Aces and finally
Total Aces, before its re-invention as Mpumalanga Black Aces.

But it is not only the smaller teams who have fallen victim to
sponsor-related name changes. Jomo Cosmos was once known
as Jomo Midas Cosmos, and Mamelodi Sundowns featured as
Shaya Sundowns. Even Kaizer Chiefs took on a sponsor's name
at one stage – playing as Iwisa Kaizer Chiefs –a move which left
them accused of virtually selling their soul! The formidable
teams of the white National Football League (NFL), Highlands
Park and Durban City, were called Dion Highlands and Sanyo
Durban City respectively. Even the once fiercely independent Dynamos had to bow to capitalism, featuring as Jade East
Dynamos for a while.

Some current teams still have sponsorship names associated
with their team names, for example, Engen Santos, Bidvest
Wits[48] and SuperSport United.

Two things in a local fan's kit make attending a soccer match
in South Africa especially unique: the trumpeting sound of the
vuvuzela and hearing fans shout the praise names bestowed

on players. The passion with which soccer fans follow specific players is reflected by the stars' nicknames. We can hardly appreciate the local soccer scene and supporters' enthusiasm without understanding something about the importance of praise singing in black culture and tradition, how the nicknames originated and what they mean. In most cases, the names comment on the player's mannerisms or some aspect of his playing style, or actions on or off the field. Sometimes a name is simply a corruption of a word by an illiterate fan.

The tradition of nicknames for soccer players is rooted in the black African culture of praise singing. Praise names carry deep cultural meaning and play an important role in African culture. As every African clan has a praise name that is used in spiritual rituals, the names have profound meaning in African traditions. Among a soccer team's 'family' the sometimes rhythmic, drumbeat repetition of the nicknames and praise names for players lends soul to the game. Each name seems to celebrate, in African style, some aspect or attribute of a player, evoking a glorious moment, either in the present or in the past, of such a player. It is meant to inspire bravery and to spur players on to greater achievements and better performance during battle. Nothing could be more fitting as the players take on each other in the serious business of soccer combat!

In the past nicknames given to players unquestionably strengthened the relationship between players and the fans, and bonds were created that otherwise would not have been established. In those days players were seen as almost belonging to communities. Walking down a township street, a player would often hear the rising shout of his nickname and soon be invited to the fan's home for a drink or two; the friends of the lucky supporter would never hear the end of that story.

The story about an African American preacher's excitement

upon spotting Ace Ntsoelengoe enter his church illustrates the almost unbelievable buzz that a star player's presence evokes. While playing professionally in the United States, Ntsoelengoe apparently once quietly entered a church after the sermon had already started. The presiding preacher, who was a fan of Ntsoelengoe's team, was in full cry, bellowing his message: 'And Jesus said . . . and Jesus said . . .' But when he saw Ntsoelengoe enter, he forgot all about what Jesus said and excitedly interrupted his sermon: 'Aaaaaace!'

Ntsoelengoe and other players who played in the States during the same time often recounted the story. Even if slightly exaggerated, it endures because many fans held Ntsoelengoe in high regard. He spent eleven seasons in America and was inducted into the American Soccer Hall of Fame in 2003 for his contribution to the development of soccer in the region.

In the fifties and sixties in particular, players' nicknames often reflected social commentary related to the political struggle of the time. Orlando Pirates defence stalwart Don 'Saracen' Ngwenya earned his name from the armoured military vehicle used in black townships at the height of police and Defence Force activity during the apartheid era. Teammate 'Black Sash' Mazibuku was named after a predominantly white liberal organisation that protested over matters like the Pass Laws by lining the streets with protestors, mostly women, each wearing a black sash.

Ben 'Walk Tall' Khule was named after the popular Cannonball Adderley jazz classic, *Walk Tall, 74 Miles Away*, which encouraged blacks to remain proud, no matter how difficult things were. '*Asina mali, asi badali*' (we don't have money, so we won't pay) was often used to refer to Kaizer Chiefs midfield maestro Jackie Masike. The phrase, a resistance slogan shouted during rent and bus boycotts triggered by tariff increases in the 1950s, reflected his tough resistance in defence and midfield.

'Aarah', the nickname of Samuel Gumede, originated from a password township residents used to warn neighbours that the police were on the prowl conducting contraband (mostly illicit liquor) or pass raids. The message of impending raids would be relayed over fences from one yard to the next. Houses would hurriedly be cleaned up, any sign of liquor destroyed, and a sense of innocence assumed for the police.

But there are also more light-hearted nicknames inspired by political structures. In 1967, Katlehong Young Zebras defender, Steve Maseko, was reportedly spirited away from his home one Friday afternoon by the notorious Brixton Murder and Robbery Squad – or rather, people who purported to be policemen. His frantic family could not believe that he could be involved in crime. It turned out that soccer boss, Uncle Dave Motsamai of Black Pirates, had arranged the 'arrest' to get the player into his camp. Not surprisingly, when he turned up for a Black Pirates game that weekend, his nickname was coined: Brixton!

The prominent place soccer occupied in the lives of blacks during the fifties and sixties is evident in some of the nicknames inspired by pop culture and contemporary events. There were several 'Buicks' and Mike Ntombela was known as 'Nanana', the name given to small cars. The pop song *Who's fooling who?* inspired Thomas Hlongwane's nickname, and similarly the song *Groovin'* (having fun) was the reason behind Groovin' Molope's name. Sullie Bhamjee was nicknamed 'Bump Jive' after the dance craze that swept the townships at the time. Even one of the best known Pirates, Eric 'Scara' Sono, earned his nickname in this way. Scara was short for 'Scaramouche', the legendary pirate in movies popular at that time – quite different from the classic definition that suggests a cowardly braggart!

Among the black community horse races were, and still are, extremely popular. Millions are wagered on horse racing every race day and the premier horse racing event in South Africa, the Durban July Handicap, carries even greater attraction. In 1971 a horse named Wagga Wagga attracted particular attention and Leonard Likoebe was promptly given the nickname 'Wagga Wagga' to celebrate his blindingly fast sprints down the field.

But mostly players were named for their playing style. The defence of Isaac 'Rocks' Mothei was, well, rock solid, as was that of Johannes 'Yster' Khomane and Jeremiah 'Ntsimbi' Gumede (*yster* and *ntsimbi* mean iron in Afrikaans and Zulu respectively), and many other defence players were given the praise name '*Ayigobeki Lentsimbi*' (this iron rod does not bend). Salthiel 'Bomber Mzioni' Chochoe and Tiger Motaung were combative and tenacious, ferocious even, on the field. Stanley 'Screamer' Tshabalala earned his name from his trademark scream when he received the ball. Kenneth 'The Horse' Mokhojoa was given this name because of the fierce power of his kicking boot.

A fetch-and-carry kind of midfield player (today better known as a playmaker) was often referred to as '*Waya, wa Buya*' (he goes forward and then falls back), which was later distorted to 'Wire'. Aaron 'Roadblock' Makhathini was a veritable obstacle for attackers. Percy 'Chippa' Moloi (the reason for the spelling is not known) was known for the easy manner in which he chipped the ball over defences to his striking partner, Alfred 'Russia' Jacobs, while Owen 'Rubber Doll' da Gama contorted his body as he wove his way past defenders. Peter 'Fuduwa' Mokotedi's nickname means 'someone who stirs' as he often made a stirring motion while dribbling past opposition.

There is much debate as to the origin of the name of soccer legend Kaizer 'Chincha Guluva' Motaung. Some say that when he was brought into the first team from the lower division by Orlando Pirates captain at the time, Eric 'Scara' Sono, the young

Motaung seemed to have had a bout of stage fright and often held on to the ball for too long. A fan who obviously did not know the player, began to shout '*Chincha wena guluva!*' ('Change, you loafer!'), meaning he should pass the ball. Another nickname that stuck owing to a fan's enthusiastic cheering is Zacharia 'Maria Maria' Lamola. The supporter reputedly asked who the amazing player in the Orlando amateur team for which Lamola played, was. In the din of the cheering, he was told the player's name was 'Zacharia'. He probably heard it as 'Maria', which he promptly started shouting. Others picked it up, and the rest is history.

Pretoria boy Bernard 'Dancing Shoes' Hartze was known for waltzing past defences with consummate ease. Other Pretoria greats whose playing style was also compared to dance moves were Lexi 'Magic Feet' Mathobela, Lucas 'Masterpieces' Moripe, and Elias 'Shuffle' Mokopane. Patrick 'Let Them Dance' Molala really made defenders dance. Thomas 'Zero' Johnson was also known as 'Gida' Johnson because he would execute the Zulu war dance, known as *ukugida*, as he challenged defenders. Opposition players found this quite intimidating!

And then, of course, there was Stephen 'Kalamazoo' Mokone, who developed his dribbling skills at Pretoria Home Stars before joining Shooting Stars at Adams College and went on to play for Durban Bush Bucks. Kalamazoo referred to the well-known Putco buses that formed the backbone of black public transport in the city – their movement a symbol of power and authority.

Some names were based on the age or physical appearance of players when they first starred for their team. Nelson 'Teenage' Dladla, Johannes 'Big Boy' Kholoane, Johnny 'Magwegwe' Mokoena (meaning bowlegged), 'Junior' Ngobe, Daniel 'Vader' Mophoso (father), or Vincent 'Last Born' Makroti, who happened to be the youngest player on the field for his team, Benoni United, are all examples.

Almost every team had a 'Terror' or 'Troublemaker', owing to the fear their style instilled in the opposition team. One of the best known 'Terrors' was politician and former South African Minister of Defence, Mosioua Lekota, whose name from his soccer-playing days stuck into his political career in later years.

Owing to all the trouble he posed to opposing teams' defences, Jomo Sono was often nicknamed 'Troublemaker'. Pretoria Callies' version of a terrorising player was Patrick Dibetla, known as 'Frelimo' because he terrorised the opposition's attacking players just like the Mozambican liberation movement did the Portuguese. Jerry 'Legs of Thunder' Sikhosana was so known for his fearsome shots at goal.

Other players' game was simply too hot to handle: 'Pele Pele' Mkhwanazi (derived from peri-peri), 'Pepper' Moloi and 'Chilliboy' Koloba.

Fulfilling the important role they do, goalkeepers are often the target of fans' praise. Goalkeepers were often called 'Black Cat' in reference to their agility, but also perhaps as a symbol of bad luck – for the opposition! Another popular name for goalkeepers was 'Never My Love', which reverberated in the stadiums each time the keeper made a save, suggesting they would always deny opposition strikers goals. Zacharia Mahlatsi and Swallows' Abraham Meyers were both known as 'Al die Hoekies', because they indeed managed to cover 'all the corners'.

Other players again were bestowed with the dubious honour of nicknames that were less than complimentary at first, but eventually stuck as fans became accustomed to their style, for example, 'Lazy Bones' Sono, 'Slow' or sometimes even 'Stadig My Kind' Masuku, just as a parent would caution a child to calm down, because Masuku often hurried his game and subsequently lost the ball. A player of more recent times, Jabu Pule, is known as 'Ngwana wa Tshwenya' (this child is naughty), because he much prefers parties to training sessions.

International names also found their way into the South African scene. Many players whose first names were George were given the nickname 'Best', after legendary English player George Best. Joseph 'Banks' Setlhodi was named after English goalkeeper Gordon Banks. A few defenders also took up the name 'Nobby Stiles' after the legendary English central defender. Following the 1966 World Cup, during which the Russian goalkeeper Lev Yashin made such an impression, many goalies came to be known as 'Yashin'.

But not surprisingly, the most popular imported name was Pele, with many players given this name also adopting the Number 10 jersey the Brazilian made so famous. The most prominent of the Pele-doubles was probably the Namibian, Herman Blaschke, who played for Kaizer Chiefs during the early 1970s.

However, just as South African players sometimes imported nicknames, so too players and their nicknames were exported. Stephen 'Kalamazoo' Mokone became the first South African player to play professional soccer in Europe and was known as 'De Zwarte Meteor' (The Black Meteor) while playing for Dutch club Heracles. Earning £10,000 a year by 1958, 'Kala' was indeed South Africa's first soccer superstar. Albert 'Hurry Hurry' Johanneson, a Germiston lad, followed in Mokone's steps by playing for English club Leeds United and becoming the first African to play in an FA Cup final, featuring for Leeds against Liverpool.

But the best-known South African soccer export is certainly Lucas 'Rhoo' Radebe. He played for Leeds United for more than ten years, including captaining the team. His fans in Leeds aptly nicknamed him 'Chief'.

It is interesting that white players who turned out for black teams usually went without nicknames. In the 1980s and early 1990s Witbank Aces had a whole array of white players – mostly from South America – including Pio Noguera, Sergio Novoa, Roberto Bitencourt and Alberto Cano and coaches Walter Rautmann, Augusto Palacios and Walter Moreira – who were never called anything other than the names on their passports, perhaps because the names didn't lend themselves to the culture of praise singing.

There were a few exceptions, of course. Bafana's Africa Cup of Nations winning captain, Neil Tovey, was known as 'Mokoko' (cock), because when running, his head bobbed in a pecking motion just like that of a cock. Other white players who did get nicknames were Andy 'Jesus' Karajinsky (because of his beard), Gavin 'Stability' Lane (after the police unit used during political unrest) and 'Brixton Tower' Jordaan, the towering Chiefs defender. AmaZulu player George 'Madlinyoka' Dearnaley's nickname means 'he who eats snakes'. Most rural Zulu people do not eat fish, and likened it to snakes. During that time, whites were known as 'Maja Tlhapi' (those who eat fish).

White players' surnames have also often been used as praise names. Mamelodi Sundowns central defender, Matthew Booth, is one of the latest examples, with shouts of 'Booooth!' every time he clears the ball or makes a significant tackle. Mark Fish was similarly cheered with shouts of 'Fiiiiish!'.

Not even administrators escaped the soccer public's witty tongues. Many were flamboyant and rich people, like Elijah Msibi, known as 'Stetson Phansi', because of his affinity for Stetson hats and shoes, and the shiny Chevrolet Impala he drove – an indication of his wealth. Ewert 'The Lip' Nene was so impressed by Muhammad Ali (then known as Cassius 'The Lip' Clay) that he imitated him in predicting scores while generally talking his team, Kaizer Chiefs, up. Sports editor at the *World*, Leslie Sehume, named George Thabe 'Kid Action' because of his undertaking to shake up soccer when he took over from Bethuel 'Mr Constitution' Morolo. There were also Elijah 'Boy Baarde' Nhlapo (the bearded one), an official of Moroka Swallows who always sported a beard.

Thanks to his surname, former Bafana Bafana coach, Clive Barker, is also known as 'The Dog'. Irvin Khoza is named 'The Iron Duke' after the powerful engine that was used in General Motors' Pontiac and Chevrolet models. The name reflects not only his powerful personality, but also his being the 'engine' of soccer administration.

Sadly, the rapturous shouts of 'Aaaaaace!' (Ntsoelengoe), 'Shooooes!' (Moshoeu) or 'Shaaaaakes!' (Ngwenya) have mostly been drowned out by the monotonous trumpeting of the vuvuzela. It causes such a din that there have been requests to ban the instrument from matches, but its supporters believe it is uniquely South African and should be retained.

The vuvuzela has become part of the soccer culture of South Africa. While the design is based on the kudu horn, which was traditionally used to summon village people to attend meetings at the chief's kraal, it is now part of a fan's artillery.

It has been compared to the Mexican wave, the samba drums of Brazil and the ringing of cow bells in Switzerland. But it takes some getting used to. The noise can be quite distracting and visiting soccer fans at the 2009 Confederations Cup, and even some teams, argued that it indeed distracted players.

But FIFA President Sepp Blatter is unmoved. 'It is African culture, we are in Africa and we have to allow them to practice their culture as much as they want to,' he said when asked about the matter.[49]

A scramble to market vuvuzelas ahead of the 2010 FIFA World Cup started during the 2009 Confederations Cup and different designs are now on offer. Some, for example the Zazu, claim to have a sound more pleasing to the ear. The Zazu is designed to the shape of the kudu horn and produces a melodic sound, but is unlikely to have the same effect on South African soccer fans.

South African fans believe they can blow away the opposition with their vuvuzelas – and are determined to do so.

5

International betrayal

When South Africa won the 2010 FIFA World Cup bid in 2004, it brought an end to almost four decades of manipulation and deceit. Nelson Mandela wept, as did thousands of others, and millions went into rapturous celebrations. 'At last, at last, at last!' one fan was heard shouting. It was not only a victory for South Africa – it was also a victory for the continent.

The struggle for international recognition of South African soccer began in 1952 when FIFA admitted SAFA to its ranks despite evidence that the organisation was not fully representative of the people of South Africa. Apart from being governed by whites, SAFA also represented only white players.

In June 1952, shortly after SAFA had been admitted to FIFA, the Campaign for the Defiance of Unjust Laws was launched in opposition to the apartheid government's increasingly repressive legislation. Three years later the Freedom Charter was adopted during a meeting of the Congress of the People, held on a dusty patch in Kliptown, Johannesburg. It called for freedom for all South Africans and declared that the country belonged to all its citizens.

In the same year Dennis Brutus founded the Coordinating Committee for the International Recognition of Sport, which began a campaign against the all-white teams that claimed to represent all South Africans in international contests, yet clearly did not.

For the next four decades the international community were reluctant to acknowledge the impact of racial inequalities on South African soccer. It took several years before FIFA finally showed SAFA – later renamed FASA – the red card.

With the launch of the Suzman Cup in 1935, the first official tournament in which African, Indian and Coloured soccer teams participated, the initial steps towards inter-racial soccer were taken. However, progress towards establishing an inter-racial soccer administration was slow, not only as a result of prevailing government policies, but also because the separate race-based administrations claimed they wanted to protect their members' interests. The stubborn tug-of-war was to leave black soccer hovering in no-man's-land for the next fifteen years.

AJ Albertyn, vice-president of the South African Coloured Football Association, proposed the concept of a non-racial federation to SAAFA in 1948. Albertyn had arranged a friendly match between a black African side and a Coloured team shortly before, in an effort to realise his vision for non-racial soccer in South Africa. Two years later, these two associations agreed to form the SASF and, after the Indian association had agreed to join the organisation, was officially launched in 1951.

The government-supported Bantu associations and the white associations, however, chose to remain outside the Federation.

The SASF became the largest umbrella soccer body in the country, representing more than 46,000 players – close to 80% of all registered players in the country. The organisation was essentially still run along racial lines though, with member associations each running their separate leagues. Representative teams from each of the race groups played against each other only at the end of their season, in a competition known as the Kajee Cup.

Although the SASF had been born from extraordinary hope for the future of South African soccer, it was no magic equaliser. Access to resources such as training facilities, match venues and development funding still remained tightly under white control, even though the new body represented the majority of the soccer playing population. Despite many attempts at amalgamation, the white-governed SAFA repeatedly brushed off the Federation over the course of several years.

The SASF then decided to approach FIFA directly for recognition as the representative administrative body for soccer in South Africa. Despite its 46,000-strong membership, FIFA turned down their application, arguing that the SASF did not control all soccer in the country. How SAFA, with far fewer members, qualified for FIFA admission was unclear, but it served as an early warning to the SASF of the difficult road ahead.

The unsuccessful application only strengthened the representative soccer body's resolve to have the FIFA membership of SAFA reversed. George Singh, a Durban-based lawyer and keen soccer administrator, was at the head of the campaign. By 1954 the SASF plight had gained enough momentum to force FIFA to review the membership of South Africa. A special FIFA committee subsequently concluded that SAFA did not represent all clubs and associations in terms of Article 3 of the FIFA statutes.[50]

FIFA sent a four-man delegation to South Africa to investigate the state of affairs. After meetings with officials from both of the South African soccer bodies, they announced that SAFA indeed represented only a minority group of players and so could not be regarded as a truly national association. However, they hastily added that football segregation was a South African tradition and custom about which FIFA could do very little. They recommended that the SASF and SAFA were rather to work together towards resolving their differences. It was a hollow victory for the SASF.

In 1956 the Minister of the Interior, TE Dönges, articulated the country's formal racial sports policy for the first time. He declared that while government was sympathetic towards and anxious to help 'legitimate non-European sporting activities',[51] these activities had to take place within the policy of separate development. Each of the racial groups was advised to organise their activities separately and that there would be no interracial competitions in the country.

Although 'non-white' sportsmen from abroad would not be barred from playing against South African 'non-whites', visiting teams were urged to respect the country's 'customs'.[52] Dönges made it clear that his government would not support 'non-white' sporting activities that promoted boycotts of whites from international competitions, designed to force the country to abandon its traditional racial divisions, and that blacks wanting to travel for such purposes would not be granted travel facilities.

In a newspaper article a few years later, Mary Draper of the Institute of Race Relations pointed out that the policy was in fact just that: a policy. She argued that according to a landmark ruling of the Natal Supreme Court in 1962, it was not illegal for persons of different race groups to play football together, and as such there was no law that prohibited mixed teams from playing against each other, or with each other.[53] Mixed sport could be played on private grounds provided there were no spectators, that separate facilities were used by the different races participating, no alcohol was served, and finally that no socialising took place after the game.

Since the government resorted to the Native Urban Areas Act, the Group Areas Act and the Reservation of Separate Amenities Act to enforce their policy, the only prohibition, Draper pointed out, was in the use of club facilities if those club facilities had been designated for use by a particular race group.

On the basis of these legislative loopholes, a golf club allowed Indian golfer Sewsunker 'Papwa' Sewgolum to play in the Natal Open Tournament of 1963. Everything about him was wrong: his colour and even his golf grip. (Although right-handed, Sewgolum placed his left hand below his right on the grip.) He could not possibly win. In addition, the white contingent was led by Harold 'The Horse' Henning, a top golfer at the time. Sewgolum, however, had not been given the script. He won and, in quite a dilemma, rather than defy government policy, the club submitted him to the indignity of being presented his prize in pouring rain while white players and golf fans relaxed in the comfort of the clubhouse.

In the second half of the 1950s, SAFA was straining to hold on to its FIFA membership under mounting international pressure. In an attempt to douse feelings, they deleted all discriminatory and exclusionary race references from their constitution. The association also changed its name to the Football Association of South Africa (FASA). In 1956 the FIFA congress in Lisbon accepted the cosmetic changes that FASA had implemented, and the South African organisation retained its membership. Representatives from the SASF could not attend, since the government had, as Dönges had threatened, denied passports to the delegates.

South Africa, represented by FASA, was invited to join Ethiopia, Egypt and Sudan at the founding conference of CAF in Khartoum in 1957. FASA representative Fred Fell sat in as founder member. It did not take long for the African countries to realise that the South African racial policies would make it impossible for CAF to accommodate South Africa in the 1957 Africa Cup of Nations. At first FASA wanted to send an all-white team to the championships, and when that was turned down, opted for an all-black team, stating that a mixed team was out of the question. South Africa was disqualified.

By the early 1960s the writing was on the wall. In March 1960, blacks protesting against the Pass Laws were shot and killed in what came to be known as the Sharpeville Massacre. Both the Pan Africanist Congress (PAC) and the ANC were banned by the government, and hundreds of people arrested or banned.

In the following years a number of incidents that highlighted the ridiculous nature of apartheid followed, which contributed to the international world gaining insight into the reality that confronted the South African people. In 1960, for example, government censors banned a cinema poster for the movie *Oceans 11*, because it showed three white actors, Frank Sinatra, Peter Lawford and James Dean, walking along a Los Angeles street with a black actor, Sammy Davis Junior. The poster was only approved when Davis was blacked out. In Cape Town, pets belonging to blacks were refused kennel facilities by a national animal welfare organisation as the facilities were designated for pets belonging only to whites. The wife of Prime Minister Dr Hendrik Verwoerd also criticised white women for having black nannies take care of their children, saying that if 'white children of working mothers were cared for by blacks, it was natural that the child would develop an attachment for his black "mother" . . .'[54]

Such was the social and political context of the time and the environment in which sports had to be played. International participation steadily became more difficult for white South African sportsmen and -women. The world began to sit up and take note of the anti-apartheid struggle.

FIFA also came under increasing pressure to act against South Africa and in August 1960, the FIFA congress in Rome resolved by a 52–10 vote that 'a national association must be open to all who practice football in that country, whether amateur, non-amateur or professional and without any racial, religious, or political discrimination'.[55] FASA was given one year to comply with the resolution or face expulsion. CAF had been more decisive in its action, having expelled South Africa from the organisation.

In 1961 FIFA decided that not enough had been done to justify the continued membership of FASA, and its membership was suspended. However, Sir Stanley Rous, former president of the Football Association of England and who was sympathetic to white South Africa's FIFA membership cause, was then elected FIFA president. Rous advocated that sport organisations, and FIFA in particular, should remain outside political matters and resisted attempts to expel South Africa.

Several other international sporting bodies also held such views, thereby neatly side-stepping the thorny issue South Africa's racial sport policy presented. In 1968 Olympics president, Avery Brundage, for example, insisted that apartheid was a government policy about which the Olympic movement should not concern itself. 'We can't change the politics of any country – that's not our business,' he said.[56]

In order to be able to claim that they had made progress towards deracialising the association, FASA offered the SASF affiliation, but without any voting powers. While the SASF rejected the offer, the Bantu associations were much more open to it. Shortly after, the JBFA announced its affiliation to the white Southern Transvaal Football Association under Dave Snaier. This cleared the way for the JBFA's mother body, SABFA, to accept the associate status that FASA had earlier offered to the SASF.

The promise of stadiums, financial and coaching support, and even the possibility of foreign tours and training literature, secured the support of Bethuel Morolo, the controversial president of SABFA. With more than 250 teams affiliated to it, the JBFA was SABFA's biggest affiliate, and Morolo knew where to place his bet. The much smaller United Coloured Football Association also joined FASA on the same terms.

In 1963 Sir Stanley Rous and James McGuire led a FIFA delegation on a contrived 'fact-finding mission' to South Africa. The Bantu associations' affiliation to FASA satisfied the delegation that FASA represented all South African soccer organisations, even though the application for affiliation by the Indian association was only discussed at a meeting shortly after Rous had left.[57]

FASA had told FIFA, in protesting their suspension, that there was 'a broad consensus amongst FASA's administrators and the white population in general that international and domestic criticism of its operations was tantamount to political interference'.[58] They insisted that 'in implementing a system of sporting apartheid, it was merely abiding by the laws and customs of the Republic of South Africa'.

Not surprisingly, Rous stated in his report to the FIFA executive that 'there is no other body which can take the place of FASA [membership to FIFA]. The members of the dissident Federation [SASF] who we interviewed, would, in our opinion, be quite unsuitable to represent association football in South Africa'.[59]

At a meeting where the Third World were poorly represented,[60] FIFA subsequently lifted FASA's suspension on the recommendation of Rous. He had argued that if the suspension was not lifted, South African soccer would be severely damaged. The victorious FASA announced that it would send an all-white team to the 1966 World Cup, and an all-black team to the 1970 World Cup.

FASA's renewed membership was, however, short-lived. It was suspended again the following year at the FIFA congress in Tokyo, attended by a larger contingent of African and Asian members. When FIFA refused to lift South Africa's suspension in 1967, Morolo wrote to congratulate Rous on his re-election as president, but in his letter expressed disappointment with the decision by the FIFA executive not to lift the suspension. According to Morolo, FIFA might have hoped for 'self-withdrawal' by South Africa, which was 'a very remote circumstance'. [61]

Morolo seemed unable to understand why SABFA's affiliation to FASA didn't satisfy FIFA's requirements for a representative association. 'Mr Constitution' even went so far as to state that he had been 'forced to the conclusion that not (sic) the South African football officials have contravened the statutes [of FIFA] in any way, but that FIFA itself is moving in a direction to defeat the aims and objects of its own statutes'.[62] Morolo's aim was apparently to protect his own interests: although recognised by FASA, he was not accepted by the non-racial SASF who labelled him a stooge of the white authorities. It was in his own interest to have FIFA recognise FASA instead of the SASF.

In response to his letter, Rous said that there were some members of the FIFA executive who were 'unmovable in their attitude towards South Africa', and that he did not hesitate to inform them of his 'dislike of their attitude at each meeting'.[63] Although he had tried to get the FIFA executive to allow a European or

British team to visit South Africa to participate in the seventy-fifth anniversary celebrations of FASA[64] and also to allow youth teams from Zimbabwe to play against South African teams, he could not get the required majority.[65]

The drive to isolate South Africa grew to frenzied levels during the late 1960s and early 1970s. Voices against apartheid grew louder and foreign governments, international corporations, churches, the media, groups and individuals began to condemn apartheid. An arms embargo was imposed, financial sanctions followed and some countries refused visas to South African officials and nationals.

Following violent clashes at Twickenham during a rugby tour by the Springboks at the end of the 1960s, sport came to be seen as a lever with which to effect political change. At the height of the anti-apartheid criticism on segregated sport, a National Party Member of Parliament declared that assaults on white sport amounted to 'a declaration of war against white civilisation in South Africa'.[66] Rugby and cricket were considered white sports and the statement demonstrated how strongly white South Africans felt about rugby and cricket.

Basil D'Oliveira also added his voice to the drive, declaring that cricket could help fight apartheid. On the African continent the Supreme Council for Sport in Africa, striving for equal representation of the continent's sport in the international arena, vowed to use every means possible to expel South Africa from international sport owing to its racial policies.

Yet the international sporting community of the Western world insisted that politics and sport should not be mixed. The Gleneagles Agreement of June 1977 by the Commonwealth Heads of State discouraged sporting contact with South Africa, but it was regarded by many as a compromise agreement that did not take decisive action against South Africa. The Council of European Sports Ministers also found this a convenient subterfuge and signed a similar agreement. Such agreements echoed earlier statements from international bodies that were opposed to interfering with sport on political or racial grounds.[67]

Amidst the international back-and-forth, black South African soccer relentlessly continued its campaign for FIFA recognition. In 1972 the SASF once more applied to FIFA, who advised Norman Middleton, SASF president at the time, that the application for membership had arrived too late to be placed before the next congress in August.

FIFA explained that accepting the SASF's membership would furthermore require that FASA first be expelled, as FIFA could not register two representatives for one country. According to the world body FASA was not suspended for contravening its rules, but because of government policy. The FIFA executive therefore granted FASA special permission to have overseas teams play in the South African Games in Pretoria the following year. FIFA sought only assurance that blacks would be allowed to *watch* the games. FIFA congress approval was not necessary for such special permissions, and it was not mentioned at congress in Paris that year.

It demonstrated once more that FASA's friends in the FIFA executive were powerful enough to process executive decisions, despite their relatively weak influence in congress. The permission was retracted early in 1973, however, when it emerged that FASA had separate teams in mind for the different ethnic groups.

In June 1974 George Thabe, president of the South African National Football Association (SANFA – formerly known as SABFA), joined the white South African delegation to the FIFA congress in Frankfurt. He followed in Morolo's footsteps when he tried to argue that the FASA suspension should be lifted. Middleton, as president of the SASF, was refused a passport to attend the meeting. The South African Minister of the Interior had earlier sought an undertaking from him that he would not do or say anything that could harm South African sport. Middleton refused, calling it blackmail.[68]

At the meeting the FIFA executive rejected Ethiopia's proposal that South Africa be expelled, saying the matter could only be dealt with at the 1976 congress. Thabe returned home to heavy political criticism for his support of FASA. Media pressure forced Thabe to withdraw as a member of the multi-racial delegation that were due to travel to Montreal in 1976 as part of another desperate bid to stave off the expected expulsion of the country.

A rebel tour led by Osvaldo 'Ossie' Ardiles and Mario Kempes, reportedly organised by Thabe during his mission to Frankfurt, failed to ignite the passion of local soccer fans. The major teams – Pirates, Chiefs and Swallows – all refused to play the rebel team. This further damaged Thabe's reputation. It also gave SANFA administrator Knox Matjila, who had appeared to be a Thabe ally, the opportunity to begin a campaign to oust him. Thabe did not react kindly to it.

But the South African government's propaganda machinery was not going to take the setback of the failed rebel soccer tour lying down. They had witnessed the opposition to cricket and rugby tours, with Peter Hain leading the attack in the United Kingdom. Then Leslie Sehume, sports editor at the *World*, wrote an article in which he questioned the wisdom of Hain's approach. The London-based Committee for Fairness in Sport, almost certainly set up by South Africa and most likely from the slush fund in what later came to be known as the Information Scandal,[69] jumped at the opportunity to have a credible black person oppose Hain. They invited Sehume to challenge Hain in a television debate.

Sehume had been a well-respected sports journalist and a professional to the core. He trained young journalists such as Phil Mthimkulu (now lecturer at the University of South Africa), Siphiwe Nyanda (current Minister of Communications) and me like an army regiment: no mistakes were allowed in our copy, facts had to be checked, submissions had to be on time. No excuses.

During the debate Sehume argued that Hain had lost contact with the sports realities in South Africa. The first anyone at the newspaper heard about the confrontation was when news of the debate came through on the wires, with reports stating that Sehume had challenged Hain to walk down a township street and see how angry black people would be with him. Blacks, Sehume argued, had not made the laws which oppressed them and suffered unfairly under the sport boycott. This position earned Sehume heavy criticism – and cost him his job at *World*.

The country had gone up in riotous smoke following student unrest in June 1976, and hundreds of youths and adults – among them Chiefs star Ariel 'Pro' Kgongoane – were killed by police and armed vigilantes. Calls for the isolation of white South Africa became strident.

It therefore came as no surprise when South Africa was expelled from FIFA for failure to comply with the FIFA statutes. The congress met on 16 July 1976, exactly a month after what was to become an important day in South African history. Under João Havelange as FIFA president, FASA lost the executive support it had enjoyed under Rous. And this time, the decision was final. For the next fifteen years South Africa would be isolated from world soccer.

Later that year the government launched a new organisation, the Football Council of South Africa, in an effort to deracialise soccer. It was meant to be an umbrella body representing both black and white associations and was chaired by George Thabe. To many in the game the Football Council was simply a new version of FASA and hence the SASF refused to be affiliated to it, dispelling hopes of true unity.

By the mid-1980s political unrest was driven to a pinnacle. Student and labour unrest were the order of the day, boycotts and sanctions intensified, foreign banks called in loans and capital left the country. Violence spread between black political organisations as they jostled for political space, and battles between supporters of the ANC, PAC, Azapo and the Inkatha Freedom Party (IFP) raged. A state of emergency was declared in 1985.

The Minister of Foreign Affairs, Pik Botha, found it increasingly difficult to justify the system, famously declaring in 1986 that South Africa could be ruled by a black president in the future.[70] A few years ealier the Afrikaans newspaper *Beeld* reportedly stated: 'For the umpteenth time, we must say: South African whites must face the unpleasant fact that ours is a besieged land and that it will become even more so unless we work out a political dispensation with blacks who are ready to talk.'[71]

Howard Barrel, a former colleague at the *World* and *Weekend World*, arranged a meeting between the ANC and the leadership of the Progressive Federal Party in 1986. This ice-breaking meeting led to further meetings, particularly what came to be known as the Dakar Conference. Businessmen, academics and religious leaders were making contact with the ANC in various forms and forums. Even the government was making cautious moves towards negotiations.

In 1988 representatives from the National Soccer League (NSL) and the SASF, including Solomon Morewa and Kaizer Motaung, met the ANC in Lusaka to discuss the role of soccer in the struggle, and its future contribution. It became clear that sport in general, and soccer in particular, had to play a significant role not only in mobilisation but also in nation building and breaking down racial barriers.

By 1989 various sports leaders had met to explore the formation of a new non-racial sports body, resulting in the formation of the National Olympic and Sports Congress. Makhenkesi Stofile, Minister of Sport and Recreation in later years, Mluleki George and Krish Naidoo advocated mass mobilisation to force white sports bodies to negotiate about new democratic structures. This was to be the basis of the National Sports Congress (NSC), founded in April 1990.

Many sport organisations still remained firmly rooted in their apartheid mould. Previously all-white organisations invited black organisations to join them, rather than working towards an amalgamated structure based on equality. The truth was that the white sport organisations had the resources – both financially and infrastructure-wise – that the black organisations did not. It was only in soccer where the black organisations had demonstrable strength in numbers, although still lacking the playing facilities that the white organisations could muster.

The process to dismantle apartheid officially began in February 1990. President FW de Klerk announced the unbanning of political parties and the release of political prisoners, including Nelson Mandela. The ANC, on its part, had suspended the armed struggle and negotiations towards a democratic constitution started. The drive for international re-admission gained momentum and South Africa was welcomed back to the Olympic Games in Barcelona two years later.

In 1991 the SASF joined the South African National Football Association, the South African Sports Association and the Football Association of South Africa for renewed talks towards unity. It was finally achieved with the newly formed South African Football Association (SAFA), which is today still the national governing body of South African soccer.

In July 1992 SAFA was re-admitted to FIFA and the South African delegation was greeted with a standing ovation at a meeting of CAF held in Dakar. With their credentials now in order, SAFA arranged the country's first official international football match in decades, and the honour went to Kings Park Stadium in Durban. South Africa defeated Cameroon 1–0.

Two years later South Africans went to the polls for the first democratic elections. Following its resounding victory, the ANC began the challenge of nation building and reconciliation of a country that had been at war with itself for over a hundred years. Again the power of sport to unite people was evident. Shortly after his inauguration as the first democratically elected president of the Republic of South Africa, Nelson Mandela joined 60,000 cheering soccer fans at Ellis Park to witness Bafana Bafana take on the might of Zambia in a friendly match to celebrate Inauguration Day.

It was a historic occasion. The political transition had taken place, and now the country needed to make its return to the world of sporting nations. There was singing and dancing in the streets, and the sense of expectation was palpable. This was something the nation had not seen before. And when Mandela made his entry, the whole stadium erupted into cheers and whistles and drum beats – anything the fans could muster to demonstrate their joy and celebratory mood. We knew, at that moment, that the good promised by the liberation struggle had triumphed over evil. South Africa did not disappoint, and won the game 2–1.

Mandela had long realised the value of sport as a nation builder. Indeed, in bestowing a lifetime achievement award to Brazilian soccer star Pele, he reportedly said: 'Sport has the power to change the world. It has the power to inspire, the power to unite people that little else has . . . It is more powerful than governments in breaking down racial barriers.'[72]

The following year provided yet another milestone for South African soccer. Orlando Pirates, who had quietly been campaigning in the Africa Champions Cup[73], grafted an away win – courtesy of a solitary strike from Jerry 'Legs of Thunder' Sikhosana – to become the only Southern African club to date to have won the continental showpiece.

Earlier that year ASEC Mimosa held Bucs to a 2–2 draw in Johannesburg and it seemed a hopeless case to believe that Bucs could beat the Ivorians at home. It was termed 'Mission Impossible', but for Bernard Lushozi, Mark Fish, Helman Mkhelele, Jerry Sikhosana, Marks Maponyane, John Moeti, Gavin Lane, Edward Motale and Williams Okpara there was no such thing as impossible.

The mighty Bucs faced their biggest challenge yet. South Africans were already winding down the year in anticipation of the Christmas holidays – 16 December is traditionally the beginning of the Christmas break – but in Abidjan, Ivory Coast, Bucs ground out a 1–0 victory over ASEC Mimosa. A long punt forward by defender Mark Fish provided Jerry Sikhosana with the opportunity to score the historic goal that gave Pirates the championship.

South African soccer had, indeed, arrived.

6

No normal sport in an abnormal society

*'There are no greater lovers of true manly sport
than the people of the Cape Colony.'*
ARE BURTON – Cape Colony Today, 1907[74]

The first soccer matches in South Africa were, by most accounts, played in Cape Town and Port Elizabeth about 150 years ago. The matches featured white British civil servants and soldiers posted to the colony. One of the more famous players in those early games was John X Merriman, who became Prime Minister of the Cape in 1908.[75]

The Western Province Football Association was founded in 1891, with its headquarters at the Green Point Track. There were several league and cup competitions at the time, such as the O'Reilly Cup.[76] It was only much later that other race groups formed their own associations like the Western Province Football Union (1904) for black players and the Cape District Football Association (1929) for coloureds. The Cape Bantu Football Association was established around 1927[77], but later changed its name to the Western Province African Football Association in line with prevailing political sentiments which encouraged organisations to identify themselves as 'African', rather than 'Bantu'.

In the Western Cape soccer was seen mostly as the game of

factory workers and it was at this level that the game flourished. The Western Province African Football Association featured teams like the Rainbows, Hungry Lions, Blues, All Blacks, Zebras, Pirates and Antelopes. This association ran an annual tournament known as the Lord Clarendon Governor-General Shield.

In 1933 Coloured players formed a national association, the South African Coloured Football Association, which led the drive towards non-racial soccer. For many years several inter-racial games were played before the government stepped in. One such a match in 1955 featured a Coloured team, Western Province Association Football Board, with famous cricketer Basil D'Oliveira as captain, and Currie Cup winners, white team Western Province. D'Oliveira and his team won 5–1.[78]

While black South Africans had regularly played rugby since the 1920s, it was only from the 1960s that they started to play organised soccer in the black township Langa. The game was reportedly promoted by a white township superintendent, who was himself an ex-soccer player. The development of soccer among black Africans was to a great extent stifled by the fact that the Cape Province was declared a 'Coloured labour preference area', which meant that only Coloured labour could be employed in the region unless it could be proved that such labour was not available. The government drew an arbitrary line, known as the Eiselen Line, to demarcate the area and so limited the number of blacks that could live in the province. This line effectively divided the Cape region into east and west, but more importantly indicated where blacks could live and work, and where not.

Whereas Gauteng soccer is usually defined with reference to Orlando Pirates, Moroka Swallows and Kaizer Chiefs, the Western Cape's soccer history is built around four teams: Cape

Town Spurs, (Lightbody) Santos, Hellenic and Cape Town City. They shaped the landscape of soccer in the region and in later years, when the game turned professional, produced more international players per capita than Gauteng and KwaZulu-Natal combined.

These Cape Town teams featured variously in the white league (City), the SASL and the Federation Professional League (FPL). Cape Town Spurs won the Seven Seas League of the FPL in 1979 and 1981, while Santos was the league winner for two consecutive years (1983 and 1984). Santos also won the Quindrink League in 1986, 1988 and again in 1990, which was the final edition before the FPL dissolved. During the difficult years of poorly sponsored Federation games, it was the prolific goal-scoring of players like Basil 'Puzzy' Jansen and Farouk Khan that kept the fans in the stands. Khan won the FPL Player of the Year award in 1971.

The Western Cape has been the most prolific in producing talent for the overseas market, with Benni McCarthy one of the best-known recent exports. McCarthy started his career at Seven Stars and then moved on to Spurs, which launched his international career with teams like Ajax Amsterdam, Celta Vigo, Porto and the English Premiership side Blackburn Rovers. McCarthy remains Bafana Bafana's leading goal scorer, with 28 goals in 66 appearances.

The province has also turned out some of the most success-ful players for the national squad, including McCarthy, Shaun Bartlett and Quinton Fortune. Bartlett and Fortune both origi-nate from Cape Town's Coloured townships. Colin Gie, who used to play for Stoke City, Highlands Park and Hellenic, groomed players like Fortune. He arranged for Fortune's move to Atletico Madrid in 1996 and was involved in his transfer when he was bought by Manchester United a few years later. Gie also coached

Goalie Babsie Mampeng fists the ball away as defender Walter Sibeko goes in to support him, while Abel Modise (striped jersey) attacks during a 1951 match between the Moroka Lions and Moonlight Darkies in Alexandra.

RIGHT: The Khoza twins –
Gabriel 'Tikkie' and
Abraham 'Mainline' – in
action for Orlando Pirates.

BOTTOM LEFT AND
OPPOSITE RIGHT: Soccer
administrator Bethuel 'Mr
Constitution' Morolo ad-
dresses a SABFA meeting.
'Mr Constitution' daringly
wags his finger at another
meeting.

OPPOSITE LEFT: School
children look on in awe as
a young Steve 'Kalamazoo'
Mokone shows off his
skills.

TOP: Ewert 'The Lip' Nene signs a sponsorship deal.
ABOVE: The ever suave Nene at a Kaizer Chiefs function with Namibian Herman 'Pele' Blaschke (left) and Pius Eigowab (right).

OLDTIMERS of Bantu Sports and Wemmer Grounds will remember Samuel 'Baboon Shepherd' Shabangu, a star in the first Bucs' squad.

FOUR TITLES IN 1978

when we were deprived of the use of municipal grounds in the 60s," Ivan Khoza, Bucs' secretary said.

"We had to travel to Durban most of the time to play our matches. Once we went to Durban to play Black Aces. Our key guys then were Scara and Kaizer Motaung. After managing to get there, we realised that we did not have jerseys.

"An Indian friend lent us a set of jerseys and saved the situation. Another blow was when it was decreed that we get rid of our coloured and Indian players," said Khoza.

"We lost Bernard 'Dancing Shoes' Hartze and four other key players because of the stupid ruling," Sipho Malinga, an official, who had joined us in the Pirates boardroom, added.

Pirates have won many titles, but their best year was in 1973 when they set a still unbeaten record of winning four titles.

The last word goes to Ivan Khoza. "We didn't win a title last year, but now we are back in full swing. I can assure you that this is going to be our year once more.

"I can also tell you that like true Pirates, we will be sailing the seven seas long after many clubs have folded."

With Pirates being the oldest team in the country, Khoza can't be accused of making empty boasts.

SCARA AND JOMO— A FAMILY OF HEROES

WHEN people talk about a "chip off the old block", the phrase immediately rings a bell in the ears of the many thousand ardent followers of the oldest soccer team in the country, Orlando Pirates, and the Sono family are to the team's fans what medicine is to a sick man. It was an untimely death that deprived Pirates of one of its most skillful player at the peak of his career when Eric "Scara" Sono died in a car accident in 1964.

And his son, "Jomo" Matsitela Sono was to be groomed, curved and trimmed to size to fit handsomely into his late father's boots. Today, Jomo is the household name and a legend in his own time. An exact replica of his skillful father, who was feared by most goalkeepers during his heyday with Pirates.

JOMO (left and above) and his father Scara Sono (top left).

DRUM June 1980 59

A spread in *Drum* magazine on two Orlando Pirates legends: Jomo Sono and his father, Eric 'Scara' Sono. Sono Jnr owns Jomo Cosmos and has also coached the national team.

TOP: Percy 'Chippa' Moloi (left) and Thomas 'Zero' Johnson during a Pirates game.
ABOVE LEFT: Nigel administrator Matthews Mpahane.
ABOVE MIDDLE: Lucas 'Masterpieces' Moripe.
RIGHT: George Thabe caucuses with fellow administrators during a meeting break.

TOP: George Thabe shakes hands with Kaizer Chiefs' Ace Ntsoelengoe before a game.

ABOVE: A group of Black Springboks in the late 1970s (from left to right): Kenneth Mokgojoa, a young Lucas Moripe, Andries Maseko and Jon Lechaba.

TOP: Eric 'Scara' Sono in an attack against Moroka Swallows in the early 1960s.

ABOVE: Abdul Bhamjee (right) and George Thabe conduct a draw for the JPS Knockout Tournament. On Bhamjee's right is Cyril Kobus.

Bradley August, Emile Baron and Anele Ngcongca, who all had overseas careers and featured for the national team. Today Gie runs a youth academy in Cape Town.

In recent years, the Western Cape has become more and more competitive in the Premier Soccer League (PSL), with both Santos and Ajax Cape Town being in the title winning mix. The formation of Ajax is the result of a visionary act that saw Seven Stars and Spurs join forces as part of Ajax Amsterdam's search for youth development outside the traditional European sources. Ajax Cape Town have produced players like Steven Pienaar, who now plays for Everton, and Chelsea's John Obi Mikel, who fine-tuned his playing with the 'Urban Warriors' before moving abroad.

Two years ago the Western Cape honoured several of its former soccer stars by appointing them as ambassadors for the 2010 World Cup. These included former Bafana Bafana players Thabo Mngomeni and Duncan Crowie, David Byrne, Roger Links, Sergio dos Santos, Sugars Qinga and Mark Williams, best remembered for his two stunning late goals during the country's Africa Cup of Nations victory.

Although soccer struggled against the more popular rugby and cricket in the Eastern Cape, prominent figures such as Danny Jordaan, CEO of the 2010 World Cup Local Organising Committee, and Elrio van Heerden, who currently plays for Blackburn Rovers, hail from the region.

When Port Elizabeth was announced as one of the host cities for the 2010 World Cup, fans joyously celebrated, knowing that this would mean much-needed development for the game in the region. The new Nelson Mandela Bay Stadium, built on an empty patch that the apartheid government once used as a buffer zone between the white suburbs and the black townships, is an imposing structure that has created much excitement among young soccer players who have begun to show keen interest in the beautiful game.

In the broader political context, the Western Cape played a crucial role in realising the goal of non-racial sport. One of the strongest symbols of this dream is the ball-and-chain memorial commemorating the legacy of Basil 'Dolly' D'Oliveira, which has taken pride of place at the entrance to the Newlands Cricket Grounds in Cape Town. He was once barred from this venue because he was classified as Coloured.

Although better known as a star cricketer, Dolly also played soccer at provincial level and turned out for the 'national' Coloured XI. He made an enduring impact on the course of sports history in South Africa. After leaving his home country to take up residency and citizenship in England, he was selected to represent England for a tour to South Africa. But John Vorster, then Prime Minister of South Africa, would have nothing of it and banned the tour.

D'Oliveira's trademark response to the controversy his inclusion in the English team caused was that he was 'just trying to play cricket with the best in the world'. It became a powerful message to those who supported the white government. He will be remembered as 'the native who caused all the trouble' – not only for cricket, but sport in general. 'It [the Dolly affair] was a pivotal point in late twentieth-century politics. It led to the sporting boycott of South Africa, which is what led, as much as anything, to the fall of apartheid,' said Paul Yule, director of a movie on D'Oliveira's life.[79]

The development of soccer in the Western Cape and Eastern Cape is rooted in the principled quest for non-racial soccer. The idea for a non-racial soccer league was born in Cape Town, when AJ Albertyn of the South African Coloured Football Association tabled such a proposal at a meeting with SAAFA in 1948. Two years later the collaboration culminated in the formation of the SASF. Around the same time, poet and activist Dennis Brutus set up the South African Sports Association (SASA) in Port Elizabeth. It was one of the first organisations aimed at promoting non-racial sport and also lobbied for the isolation of white South African sports bodies.

SASA gained the support of the ANC and one of its early successes involved preventing a match against the Brazilian national team, which was scheduled to be played in Cape Town. The team management had agreed to drop their black players in order to conform to South African laws, but after SASA protested to the Brazilian government, the country's president instructed the team not to play such a game.

SASA suspended its activities following a raid on its offices in April 1960, and the subsequent banning of Brutus a year later. Its activity had, however, cleared the way for the formation of the South African Non-Racial Olympic Committee (SANROC) in October 1962, which took over the campaign for non-racial sport. With their president, Dennis Brutus, jailed in 1963, the organisation moved its offices to London. But SANROC still could not send delegates from South Africa to international conferences, as the government denied them passports. Appeals were sent to various sports organisations, including the International Olympic Committee (IOC), through the British anti-apartheid movement.

The IOC came to play an important role and took up the fight on behalf of black South African sportsmen and women. At the IOC session in Baden Baden in November 1963 the dogged perserverance of Constantin Andrianov, a member from the Soviet Union, resulted in the IOC resolving that the South African Olympic Committee be forced to must make a firm declaration of its acceptance of the spirit of the Olympic Code. It also had to convince the South African government to change its discriminatory, racial policies by 31 December 1963, or face expulsion.[80]

With SANROC driven to inactivity in exile, white sports organisations made concessions at the threat of international isolation. The government spent millions on lobby groups and rebel tours became the order of the day. Various permit systems were introduced to create space for sports to circumvent the general apartheid provisions. But once there was an improvement in international relations, the white sports bodies would renege on the undertakings they had given the black sports codes.

Campaigns striving for non-racial sport challenged attempts by white 'establishment' sport to lure black organisations into joining them with promises of facilities, sponsorship and other forms of largesse. On 17 March 1973 several sports bodies came together to form a more radical organisation, called the South African Council on Sports (SACOS). Following discussions held in the offices of NM Pather in Durban, an influential group of proponents of non-racial sport, including Pather, Norman Middleton, Hassan Howa, Morgan Naidoo and Reg Feldman, agreed that a structured front was needed for the fight against apartheid in sport. Middleton was elected as the first president and was followed by Howa five years later.

The Cape Province became the stronghold of SACOS, with the SASF playing a leading role within this umbrella body. Seven other sporting codes also joined, including the South African (SA) Swimming Federation, the SA Amateur Athletics and Cycling Board of Control, the SA Weightlifting and Body Building Federation, the SA Men's Hockey Board, the Women's Hockey Board, the SA Lawn Tennis Union and the SA Table Tennis Board. These organisations were to form the core of SACOS, whose declared aim was to mobilise sport along non-racial lines and to seek international affiliation for their codes.

SACOS also aimed to challenge what its leaders described as the unequal distribution of sponsorship, which, they argued, resulted in the unequal development of sport. It was, in fact, the imbalance in the distribution of resources that spurred Hassan Howa into taking up the fight for justice and equality. He continued his campaign for justice and fair play until his dying day.

The apartheid government, having failed to break out of sports isolation despite support from most European and North American countries, tried a new manoeuvre. Minister of Sport Piet Koornhof announced in 1973 that the government had approved the staging of open national tournaments in which the different South African 'nations' (read races) could participate on a 'multinational' basis. Koornhof declared that these tournaments would result in South Africa having 'normal sport'. Howa, then president of SACOS, immediately responded by saying that one cannot have normal sport in an abnormal society. Thereafter the phrase 'no normal sport in an abnormal society' became the slogan for the non-racial sports movement.

As part of the 'multinational' tournament the Rand Stadium, previously a whites-only soccer stadium, hosted a Black XI against a White XI (the 'black nation' against the 'white nation'), with the White XI winning 4–0 in the round robin, and 3–1 in the final. The following year, in the Embassy Multinational series, the white team beat the black team 2–0, but not before the referee had denied the black team a legitimate goal scored by McDonald 'Rhee' Skhosana. Black fans peppered the pitch with bottles and other missiles.

Soccer coach Joe Frickleton infamously declared that it would take black teams a decade to beat white teams as they were technically inferior. White journalist André van der Zwan made a similar comment in the *Rand Daily Mail*. Such comments were not surprising; South Africa was still in the grip of racial sports and social policies. Government policies had ensured that blacks and whites remained in their racial enclaves – to the extent that whites knew very little about black soccer. The rift between black newspaper reporting and white newspaper reporting was as vast as the distances between black townships and white suburbs.

Government then indicated that various changes to sports policy would be implemented in 1975, with Koornhof announcing another 'multinational tournament' for the title of Champion of Champions. Koornhof launched the Chevrolet Champion of Champions tournament with great fanfare at the Landrost Hotel in downtown Johannesburg. This was one of only a few hotels that the government had given the status of 'international hotel', which meant that blacks could receive the same treatment as whites – including being served alcohol. Other facilities remained segregated, and even at the so-called multinational games, blacks and whites could not sit together. The ridiculous nature of the policy was exposed when Jomo Sono was denied entry to the Berea Park Club recreational facilities even though he could play for the club. The club argued that if they accepted one black, they would have to accept all – a situation which they could not contemplate.

The tournament featured white teams against black teams, and Hellenic beat Kaizer Chiefs by a 5–2 aggregate score. Once more, a riot almost broke out when the referee allowed a dubious goal for Hellenic, and this incident provided fuel for those who argued that inter-racial matches were a time bomb.

While SACOS were initially not opposed to negotiating with establishment sports bodies, they virtually declared war against them by the late 1970s. SACOS viewed sport as a microcosm of society, and called not only for sports equality but also for the total abolition of apartheid.

This was evident in their 1977 resolution, later known as the Double Standards Resolution. This Resolution was aimed at stopping black sporting codes and sports leaders from engaging in multinational sport. But they went beyond sport, and SACOS banned its members from any contact with or involvement in government-created institutions like regional councils, or any other institutions that the government had introduced or funded.

The resolution followed a debate within SACOS over the relationship between the SA Cricket Board and the white SA Cricket Council, and a proposal that the two should merge. SACOS was against any merger and this position led to several defections. Two of its biggest members, the SASF and the South African Rugby Union, also felt the anger of the organisations' leadership: the SASF for applying for the use of segregated playing facilities and the Rugby Union for using hotels that had been classified as 'international' by the government and was therefore supposedly open to all races.

SACOS had earlier been accused of not including black Africans in their membership to any significant extent, but the organisation was uncompromising in its stand against what they termed 'collaboration' with apartheid structures. Similarly, the resolution affected black sports leaders who enrolled their children at white private schools following the breakdown in the education system in the black townships after the unrest of 1976. Their justification for moving their children into private schools did not get any sympathy from SACOS –

and as a result, they were barred from being part of the organisation.

In 1979, SACOS called for a moratorium on international sporting contact, urging sports organisations to suspend ties with South Africa until apartheid had been abolished. This meant that sportsmen and -women could not legitimately visit South Africa, or be visited by teams or players from South Africa.

While SACOS were leading the local fight against racial sport policies, Sam Ramsamy orchestrated the international anti-apartheid sports isolation campaign from the United Kingdom. In 1978, the United Nations had drafted an international convention called the International Declaration Against Apartheid Sport that provided for action against sports bodies and individuals who continued to make contact with or play in South Africa.

The skills that Ramsamy brought to the struggle were invaluable. Although the convention was only approved in 1985, the United Nations Special Committee against Apartheid had started the 'Register of Sports Contacts with South Africa' in 1980. Hundreds of sportsmen and -women who defied the boycott call were listed, based on information Ramsamy meticulously compiled from notes smuggled through to him in code and by couriers where newspapers did not cover events. Several countries barred those who appeared on the list.

But establishment sport continued their efforts to promote 'multinationalism' and cited the small concessions that the government had made as evidence of the country's commitment to change. Embassies put out publications highlighting these changes, and accused SACOS of being obstructionist and not representative of the majority of sports people in the country.

By 1982 SACOS had evolved into an organisation that spoke

out beyond sport and demanded a free and democratic government, stating in a resolution that the organisation would re-dedicate itself to working towards 'the total abolition of discrimination in sport and society', and striving for 'a single, undivided democratic country free of discrimination, oppression and exploitation'.[81] Their stern refusal to engage in any negotiations or discussions with government structures eventually contributed to the organisation's demise.

In the 1980s the Mass Democratic Movement engaged SACOS, urging them to build a mass-based democratic organisation. Steve Tshwete, who became a minister of sport and later safety and security in the ANC government after the 1994 elections, argued that organisations such as SACOS should prepare themselves to deal with issues in the transitional period and that it was necessary for non-racial organisations to review their strategies and policies. But SACOS were immovable in their opposition to any dealings with the government.

Alec Erwin, at the time education officer for the National Union of Metal Workers (later Minister of Public Enterprises), was among those who tried to guide SACOS towards the new approach. In delivering the annual NM Pather Memorial Lecture in 1987, he said that sport could only play a positive role in the liberation struggle if it was mass-based and democratic. He went even further – radically so in the eyes of SACOS – when he urged that the boycott of facilities should be lifted and that all individuals, including those who had previously participated or were still participating in multinational sports activities, should be engaged.

'Use or non-use of apartheid facilities is no longer a crucial political question – it does not take us forward strategy-wise,' he said.[82]

Reg Feldman, then president of the SACOS-affiliated Transvaal

Council on Sport, agreed that the boycott policy deprived blacks, but argued that sacrifices had to be made if they were 'to obtain [the] goal of a truly non-racial South Africa.'[83]

Between 1988 and 1989 various sports leaders met to explore the formation of a non-racial sports body, leading to the launch of the National Olympic and Sports Congress. This organisation met with SACOS in Cape Town and East London to explore common ground, but principle differences led to the two organisations going their separate ways.

In 1990 SACOS began to bleed to death when many high-ranking officials such as Makhenkhesi Stofile (later minister of sport), Mluleki George and Krish Naidoo left the organisation to start the National Sports Congress (NSC), which was open to negotiations with white sports bodies. Soon various non-racial sports codes began to defect from SACOS to the NSC.

As various sports leaders travelled into Africa to meet with the ANC in Lusaka and Dakar, it provided a new challenge for SACOS.

The SACOS leadership knew by then that they had to take a new approach, and in a move they believed would popularise the organisation at grassroots level, decided to prefix all the names of their affiliates with SACOS, so that their members were known as, for example, SACOS Western Cape or SACOS Transvaal. In reality, this simply served to move the chess pieces around and neither contributed to an increase in membership nor stemmed the tide of defections to the NSC.

When SACOS expelled the FPL in 1992, it signalled the beginning of the end. Perhaps in desperation, SACOS accepted the membership of SANFA, an organisation they had shunned previously because of Thabe's involvement in the community councils and the government's multinational soccer tournaments. But they had lost the membership of the SASF, which had also provided them a toehold in the African community and had give them some mass appeal.

SACOS ebbed and waned and finally drowned under the weight of its principled position.

7

Pay for play

There is nothing exceptional about Alexandra, a township in the heart of Johannesburg, sandwiched between two highways and surrounded by affluent white suburbs. For many South Africans driving between Johannesburg and Pretoria, it hardly merits a second glance.

A minister of native affairs in the early 1940s once described Alex, or Township as it is also known, as 'a running sore of evil and a place where the King's Writ runs with difficulty'. 'All the toughs and roughs and criminals congregate there,' he added.[84] During World War II jittery whites in the suburbs around Alex reportedly depicted it as 'the Mecca of native scum' and 'a main Nazi propaganda and plotting centre'.[85]

But for the people living there, Alex was more than just home. It was one of the few places where blacks could buy and own land in South Africa. Despite not having electricity, Alex was energised by its own vibrancy – the comings and goings almost continuous. Alex has for a long time truly been the 'Township of Rhythm';[86] the fun, the laughter, the life of gay abandon – these gave Township a distinctive identity.

Fifty years ago it was already a sprawling township. At the end of the working day the major bus terminus at the entrance to Alex would become a hive of activity, an unending stream of sweaty faces pouring out of the buses before they snaked down London Road. The mass of humanity would swell into the narrow streets, gingerly avoiding streams of reeking sewage overflow. Decaying waste littered the pavements – where such existed – and rickety makeshift buildings seemed to lean away from the streets as if to escape the stench carried along the stream of dirty water flowing out of the 'yards'.

Everyone in Township lived in a 'yard'. These were not yards in the conventional sense, but rather clusters of communal abodes, seemingly self-sufficient: the shebeen, the hawker who sold just about anything, the barber, the spaza shop[87] and the tailor and dressmaker. You could find almost all necessities within a yard. If not, you would find what you needed in the dark, dingy shop around the corner where you had to stop upon entering to allow your eyes to adjust, the image of an old man leaning on the counter in anticipation of a much-needed sale slowly developing.

Perhaps it was this engulfing poverty and neglect that shaped the response of the township's residents. They were proud and they owned their land, and there was money to be made by entrepreneurial exploration. Township also produced some of the country's prominent leaders and leading intellectuals, including poet Mongane Wally Serote, the late Joe Modise (former Minister of Defence) and musicians Hugh Masekela and Caiphus Semenya, among others.

It is almost ironic that the rags-to-riches tale of black professional soccer would start in one of the most neglected townships in the country – the township that no local authority wanted and nobody had ultimate authority over, the one that so many white authorities wanted to disappear.

In this unlikely setting, one of the major events of South African soccer took place. In February 1961, at a meeting held at the Alex home of Lucas Khoza, an uncle of Irvin Khoza, ten officials decided to break away from the non-racial SASF, which was opposed to professionalism. They formed the non-racial SASL that set the standard for what a professional league ought to be.

By the late 1950s the trend towards professional soccer had become prominent internationally. Journalist Vivian Granger, diamond magnate Dave Marais, and soccer administrators Lubbe Snoyman and Syd Chaitowitz launched the NFL in 1959. But this league was designated for white professional teams only. Not surprisingly, the white amateur association, FASA, opposed this move, largely because they felt threatened by the emergence of a professional league. For many in the amateur ranks, soccer was a game to be enjoyed as a leisure activity and paying players would be the thin end of the wedge, they argued.

In a desperate attempt to discourage the professional body, FASA played their trump card, barring the league from soccer grounds under FASA control – the same technique municipalities had previously used against black soccer associations who resisted their control. The premier soccer ground in Johannesburg, the Rand Stadium, and other council-owned facilities were therefore not available to the new league. Refusing the league access to grounds had little impact, however. Grounds owned by private enterprises and the South African Railways were at the disposal of the NFL and so they were able to circumvent the problem of match venues.

The league featured teams such as Rangers, who won the first NFL Castle Cup in 1959, Durban City, Highlands Park, Addington, Maritzburg, Cape Town City, Durban United, Arcadia and Hellenic. There was no shortage of competitions either: the UCT

Bowl, the TNSC Trophy, the Coca-Cola Shield and the Flood-light Bowl were among the competitions in which the teams participated.

The introduction of the professional game was responsible for instituting many changes in the South African soccer environment, not least the establishment of popular teams such as the formidable Highlands Park and the Banana Boys, Durban City. Highlands originated as a branch of the Balfour Club, which, although one of the leading Transvaal teams at the time, could not enter a side in the league owing to their amateur status. Lucke Matus, a well-respected figure in soccer circles, registered the company Highlands Park Football Club (Pty) Ltd after raising capital equivalent to R50,000.[88] The initial team included names such as Neville Scott, Basil Hauser, Leon Banducci and Gordon Frew, and for many years the club was a force to be reckoned with.

Being white, the NFL teams were able to recruit players overseas since the government welcomed white immigrants. In addition to the local boys, white players from Brazil, Scotland and former European colonies, such as Mozambique and Zimbabwe, turned out for Highlands Park. Highlands became one of the most formidable teams of the league, with their 1975 team known as the 'Mean Machine'. Many a soccer fan – black and white – fondly remembers that great Highlands Park team, which featured the likes of Freddie Kalk, Jorge Santoro, Vasco Pegado, Bobby Hume, Willie McIntosh and Stan Jacobitz.

Other international stars such as Eusébio (da Silva Ferreira), John 'Budgie' Byrne, Alan Ball, Derek Dougan and Bobby Charlton also had a run in South Africa, albeit in the twilight of their careers. Durban City boasted, over the period of its life in the NFL since May 1959, no fewer than seventeen English players, including Sir Stanley Matthews who appeared as a guest player for the side.

International players were loved by white and black supporters alike, and black soccer players who dreamt of competing with players of such standing held them in particularly high regard. Memorable games featuring Durban City and Durban United or Addington, duels between Bobby Chalmers and George Ryder, Henry Hauser's darting runs for Addington and Les Salton's 23 goals in eleven games still feature in animated recollections of those heady days. It was inevitable that calls for an 'own professional league' would soon be made.

At the same time, the principle of 'pay for play' was already being practiced by black teams, albeit informally. Teams would play for 'stakes' – an amount wagered in a winner-takes-all manner – and players often received small rewards from the club patrons for wins. Supporters also laid their own bets against each other, often leading to matches being abandoned because referees were accused of having been bribed to ensure victory by one team over another.

During the campaign for a formal black professional league, the influential role of the media in the lives of the black middle class again became evident. *Drum* magazine had established itself as an influential voice in highlighting the plight of the black community. ('When *Drum* beats, Africa listens' the magazine's slogan boasted.) Its editors became aware of the desire for a professional league among black soccer fans. They argued that whites were mostly interested in rugby and cricket, while soccer was predominantly enjoyed by blacks. The fan support for clubs proved that soccer was the number one sport for black South Africans.

Following the potato boycott after the Bethal Potato farm

scandals were exposed,[89] *Drum* added the need for a professional body for black soccer to the list of causes for which it campaigned. Soccer administrator Dan Twala, community leader
Job Rathebe, who was dubbed the 'most popular man on the
Reef', and former ANC President Dr AB Xuma, were even appointed to the magazine's editorial board to advise owner Jim
Bailey and editor Anthony Sampson on how they could better
serve their readership.[90]

In February 1961 the first steps towards introducing professionalism to black soccer were taken at the Alexandra meeting.
When the meeting adjourned, it was triumphantly announced
that a professional body for black soccer had been formed,
namely the SASL. Led by RS Lutchman, president of the Durban
Indian Football Association, and Dan Twala, then president of
JAFA, the SASL was to become one of the best professional soccer leagues of the time.

The SASL soon established itself as the top professional
league in the country, drawing thousands to non-racial soccer
encounters. Black, Indian and Coloured teams belonged to the
league. Although white teams had been invited, they rejected
the offer. The league had also established a relationship with
SANROC, which operated out of London after being banned
in South Africa. The SASL proved to critics of non-racialism
that inter-racial soccer was not only possible, but also popular
and desirable. Its success led to it being targeted by government and municipal officials as the organisation adhered to
non-racialism and refused to bow to the racial prescriptions of
the government.

The SASL kicked off featuring Avalon Athletic, Berea and
Aces United from Durban, Moroka Swallows, Transvaal United
and Blackpool United from Johannesburg, and Cape Ramblers
from Cape Town. Orlando Pirates initially did not join the

league. With several divisions registered with the JBFA as Sea Robbers, they had access to stadiums allocated to the JBFA by the Johannesburg Council, and it was more profitable to remain neutral and play gate-taking friendly matches all over the country. Irvin Khoza, who now effectively owns the club, recently said that this probably helped to build the club into a national brand. As the SASL grew in stature and drew large crowds to their fixtures, Orlando Pirates, Maritzburg City, Lincoln City and Durban Hearts joined the league in its second year.

The SASL teams used the Curries Fountain grounds in Durban and the Green Point Track in Cape Town – none of which fell under control of the Non-European Affairs Departments of the respective city councils. In Johannesburg the only available venue was the Natalspruit Indian Sports Ground near the Jeppe Men's Hostel, which soon became synonymous with good, high quality soccer.[91]

Not even the painfully inadequate facilities could dampen the enthusiasm of players, officials or fans. The Natalspruit stadium was always packed as fans jostled to see the likes of the daring Avalon Athletics forward Dharam Mohan, Conrad Stuurman, Eric 'Scara' Sono, Difference 'City Council' Mbanya, King Kaizer 'Matatazela' Mkhwanazi and Joseph 'Carlton' Moloi strut their stuff. In 1964 one of the most influential players in the SASL, Eric 'Scara' Sono, tragically died in a car accident aged only 27. He was the father of Jomo Sono.

Meanwhile, the white NFL was also firmly established and, owing to the support of Dave Marais, who had won a parliamentary seat in the all-white elections of October 1961, had full access to all white facilities. The league excluded blacks, who, even as spectators, were allowed only into small corners, away from the white fans. The Durban teams had significant Indian support, but even they were relegated to one area of the ground. With the threat of international isolation looming, the NFL were forced to review their race policies, but decided to retain their whites-only status.

However, one of the league's founders, Vivian Granger, hatched a strategy to co-opt blacks by launching a professional association for blacks as an appendage to the white NFL as competition to the SASL. A group of Africans, led by Seth Mzizi and Sidney Sepanya, were brought in and the National Professional Soccer League (NPSL) was founded. At the same time, in 1961, SASA had launched an operation they termed Support Only Non-Racial Events in Sport, which campaigned for the boycott of associations supported by government or white groups. The league subsequently did not get the support of the major teams. The boycott of the NPSL quickly led to its demise.

Two years later black teams, mostly from the Transvaal and not affiliated to the SASL, decided to launch the Transvaal Professional Soccer League. It announced itself as a national league and was soon renamed the South African National Soccer League (SANSL). It was not difficult to recognise the hand of Marais and Granger in this league. Marais promised to inject vast sums of money into the SANSL: at the launch a sponsorship of an unprecedented R50,000 was pledged, with further sponsorship expected from FASA.

Confident that this would attract the black associations, Marais and Granger went ahead to set up fixtures for the new league. They held discussions with individual clubs to get their support, but made the mistake of not consulting with Bethuel Morolo, president of SABFA. At one meeting I covered for the *World*, a SABFA delegate described Granger as 'a snake in the grass', accusing him of bad faith for trying to negotiate with individual clubs. League matches were severely delayed. Marais and Granger's plans for a national professional league were scuppered by Morolo. To increase his power and influence over soccer, Morolo, of course, wanted such a league to be a unit of SABFA as a direct affiliate.

The success of the SASL encouraged Morolo and his supporters to get a professional league under way. New life was breathed into the NPSL, this time with the knowledge of SABFA, and Sidney Sepanya was subsequently appointed as secretary. Assuming he had the authority to do so, Sepanya issued fixtures for the NPSL's championship called the Castle Shield.

But at an extraordinary meeting of the SABFA executive, it was pointed out that SABFA had planned to run zonal eliminations first to determine the clubs for the league.[92] Coloured and Indian associations were supposed to do the same and recommend teams to the league, which was meant to include both Indian and Coloured teams, before the NPSL could kick off. Continued bickering and disagreement over the inclusion of Coloureds and Indians meant that the league was grounded once more.

Attempts to amalgamate the SANSL (conceived by Granger and Marais) and the NPSL (the brainchild of Morolo and SABFA) failed dismally. Clubs continually pledged their support to one league and then crossed over to the other as soon as prospects looked better on that side. On both sides officials believed their privileged positions would be threatened by any attempt at unity and in the end. the league neither got off the ground nor did the unity effort succeed.

Marais's frustration with black teams who would sign up with the SANSL but then not turn up for matches prompted him to try a different approach. The white NFL tried to co-opt SABFA by wooing them with the idea of an 'airborne league':

flying teams to venues in Durban and Cape Town, instead of them having to travel by rail or road. While the plan looked attractive, the major clubs such as Orlando Pirates saw this as an attempt to reimpose white control on soccer and refused to be party to this.

To further compound the confusion and mistrust, SABFA relaunched the NPSL for a third time, now for black African teams only. But the organisation was beset with administrative problems, despite financial support from sponsors, and competitions were often in disarray. NPSL fixtures featuring clubs such as Black Pirates, Katlehong United, Benoni United, Spa Sporting Club and Black Birds simply could not compete with the attraction freelance matches involving Orlando Pirates or Moroka Swallows offered and failed to draw significant crowds. At one stage corruption charges were brought against NPSL soccer leaders, including Morolo, with the officials accused of misuse of sponsored funds. The case was heard in the Johannesburg Magistrates Court, but the charges were withdrawn after conflicting evidence was led.

Although the SASL games had proved popular with the fans, the league struggled to keep afloat as bureaucratic pressure mounted. The Group Areas Act, the Separate Amenities Act and the State Security Act were all used to persecute the organisation. In Durban, SASL side Lincoln City, who had white, Indian and Coloured players in their team, were prosecuted for violating the Group Areas Act in 1962. The judge found that, although the players had played together, they had not entered any building together, socialised or shared refreshments – as stipulated by the act. But it did not stop the authorities from continuing their attack on the SASL: the security police went so far as to attend SASL meetings and take notes.

In Johannesburg the SASL were finally denied access to the

famous Natalspruit Indian Sports Grounds, possibly under in-
stigation of the white NFL and Dave Marais, who was a city
councillor by that time. Fans, however, were not deterred when
the goalposts were removed, and promptly found and trans-
ported goalposts to the ground to ensure that a particular match
went ahead. In April 1963, on the day of one such match, 15,000
fans watched Alexandra Real Fighters and Transvaal United
battle it out (Fighters 1, United 0), followed by Moroka Swallows
thumping Blackpool United 6–1. Double-headers were common because of the lack of facilities.

Granger and the manager of the NEAD in Johannesburg,
William Carr, worked together to stop SASL sides from gaining
access to grounds. Government also stepped in and sent a di-
rective to municipalities stating that 'all stadia and fields for
native football . . . [were] reserved for use by associations affiliated to the Football Association of South Africa'.[93]

Not even the most enthusiastic support from fans could save
the ailing SASL. Efforts to use the Kliptown Sports Grounds
were futile and it soon became clear that the end was nigh.
Rodgers Sishi cut a lonely figure on the touchline during one
of the last games of his team, Alexandra Real Fighters, at the
dusty venue.

Increasing government pressure and the lack of facilities as
the Group Areas Act pincer tightened, forced clubs to review
their position if they were to survive. When neither Orlando
Pirates nor Moroka Swallows signed up for the league in 1965, it
was the final nail in the coffin. By April of that year, the league
had still not kicked off and the chairman, Big Boy Haffejee,
was pressured to resign. A special meeting, at which he was
to advise the press of his intended resignation, was called.

Overlooking vice-chairman Dan Twala, who should have
taken over automatically in terms of the league's constitution,

the meeting proposed SK Naidoo as succesor. Haffejee, however, decided not to resign. The Transvaal delegation, led by Cyril Kobus, subsequently put forward a motion that should Haffejee resign in future, Twala would automatically take over. The motion was defeated, and the Transvaal delegation, including Twala, walked out. It was the end of non-racial professional soccer.[94]

Clubs such as Pirates and Moroka Swallows again resorted to freelancing, playing against various Invitation XI teams. This became quite a profitable exploit for teams that could muster big crowds. A simple hessian sacking fence strung around the pitch sufficed where proper facilities did not exist, and with fans virtually lining the touchlines, teams managed to keep soccer going.

In 1969 the Swaziland government invited Highlands Park and Orlando Pirates to feature in a game at the official opening of the newly built Somhlolo Stadium near Mbabane and as part of the country's independence celebrations. The game presented a prime opportunity to promote inter-racial sport. Neither FASA nor the NFL objected to the planned game. Pirates had, however, registered their second team, Sea Robbers, with the JBFA in a complex arrangement that gave them access to municipal grounds. In the eyes of the JBFA and SABFA, the club therefore had to seek the permission of both organisations; Pirates, on the other hand, didn't deem it necessary. SABFA president Bethuel Morolo felt snubbed.

SABFA argued that Bucs should not be allowed to play against Highlands Park, as such a game would not, under prevailing conditions, have been allowed in South Africa. They argued that it would have made a mockery of the law if the game were allowed to take place. SABFA's argument was enough to convince the South African government to ban the game. Morolo had shown over the years that it was his way or the highway – regardless of how much soccer suffered in the end. Since it would have been a FIFA-sanctioned game, the decision dealt a significant blow to FASA's reputation in the international soccer community, despite high-ranking FIFA friends.

With the SASL grounded, SABFA retained almost sole control over the course of black professional soccer through the NPSL. In 1971 George Thabe, who had earlier taken over from Bethuel Morolo, announced new constitutions for both SABFA and the NPSL. A new fixture list and programme for an 'airborne' league were drawn up. SABFA also launched the Keg League (later renamed the Castle League),[95] supported by a South African Breweries (SAB) sponsorship of around R30,000 that had been obtained with the help of Dave Marais.

In 1977 the white NFL eventually dissolved, thereby sounding the final whistle for many white teams and individual players. Those who did not want to hang up their boots joined teams such as Dynamos, Lenasia Swaraj, Bluebells, Durban City, Verulam Suburbs, Cape Ramblers, Aces United and Cape Town Spurs in the FPL. The once formidable Highlands Park also felt the crunch and the club's fortunes waned considerably. Jomo Sono showed his business acumen when he bought the ailing Highlands Park from the dying NFL and renamed it Jomo Cosmos.

Professional teams now had only two options: to join either the NPSL or the non-racial FPL, which was set up by the Indian and Coloured teams from the folded SASL.

The Castle League became the dominant league, and when the SABC broadcast its first soccer game on television and then also live games in 1981, the NPSL had even more leverage to raise sponsorships. The NPSL became rather wealthy, with revenue soon reaching the R8 million mark. The addition of a second television channel, which screened a 'Match of the Day' as well as the day's live broadcast, earned the NPSL a further R250,000 from boradcasting rights, ensuring the financial success of the league. It was inevitable that companies would see the marketing opportunities and by 1982, SAB had increased its sponsorship to R325,000.

Not even the lure of all these sponsorships could successfully unite professional soccer; in fact, it only added more controversy. The next scene in the drama that professional soccer had become was set when Thabe's SABFA leadership was challenged during the 1986–7 season, specifically because he held the top position at both the NPSL and SABFA. Clubs began to demand autonomy for the NPSL, which was run and controlled by SABFA at the time. Discontent also rose because clubs were not represented on the NPSL Committee. Eventually two club representatives – Sylvester Masinga from Moroka Swallows and Agrippa Mbathani from Orlando Pirates – were appointed to a new committee known as the NPSL Management Committee.

Thabe's involvement in apartheid civic politics such as the government-created Vaal Triangle Community Council and his perceived support for so-called multinationalism, the apartheid government's tainted version of multiracialism, were seen as compromising both the NPSL and SABFA in their relations with political organisations. Thabe believed that Abdul Bhamjee, who was then the public relations officer of the NPSL, was responsible for a simmering rebellion. Thabe shocked the soccer world when he announced Bhamjee's expulsion from the NPSL at a press conference in 1989 – with an unsuspecting Bhamjee attending. This event triggered Thabe's demise.

Bhamjee retaliated by bringing together officials Kaizer Motaung, Cyril Kobus and Irvin Khoza to lead a breakaway from the NPSL. The sweetener, for many, was that they planned to run a professional league in the mould of the defunct SASL. With the support of Solomon Morewa, secretary of the powerful Transvaal Football Association, and his president, Leepile Taunyana, the NSL was formed. All the major teams – except Moroka Swallows – joined. Taunyana, who was also an official of SABFA, was elected chairman of the new organisation – and as reward was promptly suspended by an irate Thabe.

Having mustered the leading teams, the NSL immediately won the support of sponsors. Bhamjee, Kobus and Motaung approached SAB with their long-term vision for soccer in South Africa. SAB agreed to support the league to the tune of R400,000.

The NPSL was left mainly with amateur teams and various versions of the major professional teams, leading to legal tussles over the use of names. Clubs that had not been registered previously were hastily registered to protect their names. The breakaway NSL divided teams, including Orlando Pirates. In one demonstration of the depth of the rifts, fans saw China Hlongwane, who led one faction of Pirates, being stabbed several times on live television.

It was a shocking sight, one that will hopefully not be seen on television again. Hlongwane, who was a big man, staggered around the ground as he was being pursued, with the knife finding its mark several times. The stabs were meant to kill, but Hlongwane survived and lived for years after that day in 1985. He often boasted that he wouldn't die easily.

Swallows' Aaron 'Roadblock' Makhathini was shot and killed outside his home returning from a training session. It was reported at the time that his death was related to the ongoing fights over affiliation to the new NSL. Two top Swallows officials were arrested in connection with the murder, but no evidence was found to charge them.

The volume of newspaper coverage of the league's activities was critical to its success and moreover, its ability to attract sponsorships. Bhamjee realised it would be an issue of how he positioned his new organisation, and how the support of the largest number of journalists could be won. Allegations that Bhamjee offered some journalists bribes, including heavily discounted motor cars, later emerged.

This was a major blot on sports journalism generally, but more specifically brought to the fore the dangers of journalists getting too close to the subjects of their reporting. Some sports writers' careers were almost ended, others' badly derailed. The sports editor of the *Sowetan*, which replaced the *World* when it was closed down by the government, was demoted to a junior reporting position for accepting one such motor car deal and so compromising the newspaper and its sports coverage.

These events dramatically changed the face of South African soccer. The idea of the Charity Spectacular was born during these turbulent times, largely as part of the strategy of Kobus and Bhamjee to consolidate the position of the NSL and also to improve perceptions about soccer administration. LM Mathabathe, a great supporter of soccer, was a senior employee of Premier Milling, which wanted to get involved in soccer. At Mathabathe's encouragement, the company jumped at the new opportunity by sponsoring the Charity Spectacular under their Iwisa maize meal brand.

Journalists competed with each other for newly introduced awards, and the concept of regular press conferences with sure television coverage was introduced for major announcements.

This has ensured that all journalists get an equal bite at any major announcement, although information is still leaked to journalists ahead of announcements. Journalists across the world find cultivated contacts useful.

Controversy hit South African soccer once more when the government appointed a commission of inquiry into allegations of corruption in soccer in 1996. The Pickard Commission exposed corruption and mismanagement in the top flight of soccer. Solomon Morewa, as president of SAFA, was found to have had a corrupt relationship with Brian Mahon, head of a sponsorship and marketing company to whom Morewa had virtually sold the country's soccer rights. In return, he had received a luxury German car and R500,000 deposited into his personal account. The commission recommended Morewa be dismissed and proposed several changes to the NSL's governance structures.

The NSL took soccer to a new level with the launch of the eighteen-team PSL in 1996, a process in which Kaizer Motaung, Irvin Khoza, Jomo Sono and Raymond Hack played a significant role. The league was later reduced to sixteen teams because of fixture congestion. The franchises of two teams, Ria Stars and Free State Stars, were bought out for R8 million each and the clubs were disbanded.

A new management structure, consisting of a board of governors, was set up. This was meant to take professional soccer away from the control of SAFA to align it with other similar structures around the world, most notably the English Premier League.

Irvin Khoza and Kaizer Motaung both realised that soccer needed to be developed generally if their own teams (Pirates and Chiefs respectively) were to achieve greatness. They gradually built the brand of the PSL by ensuring that sponsorships and other competitions were commensurate with the value of the league. Multimillion rand sponsorship agreements were signed, including a major television deal with pay-television channel SuperSport.

In 2004 yet another controversy hit the league when a match-fixing scandal rocked South African soccer. The South African Police launched an investigation code-named 'Operation Dribble' in June and more than 40 arrests were made, ranging from club bosses to match commissioners and referees and their assistants. Almost all the cases were withdrawn because of lack of evidence, leaving only four people, said to be the 'small fish', to be convicted of attempting to influence the outcome of games. The fanfare with which this investigation was announced turned out to be a damp squib, which raised suggestions that there had been a cover-up and that the truth had not emerged. It was not the first time such views were heard: the report of the Motimele Commission, which probed corruption in South African soccer as far back as 1999, was never made public despite calls for it to be published.

British administrator Trevor Phillips was brought in to structure the PSL. His experience as an official in the English Premiership got the organisation off to a good start. But soon he began to tread on the toes of members of the Board of governors, whose interests were largely with their own clubs. An array of administrators followed, but eventually Phillips was brought back to manage the PSL to its best performance yet. When he resigned in 2007, Norwegian Kjetil Siem was appointed as Chief Executive Officer.

What once was a game in which players were rewarded with an orange rolled up to them during the half-time break, has today become a launch pad to a world of staggering riches.

Stephen 'Kalamazoo' Mokone writes in his autobiography that soccer provided an escape for him and other young blacks.[96] It plucked him from the poverty of Atteridgeville, west of Pretoria, where he played for Home Stars, and took him to Amanzimtoti on the KwaZulu-Natal north coast, where soccer fame and fortune followed. And when he became the first black South African player to sign international contracts (Coventry City, Heracles and Torino amongs others), he really found himself in the riches.

Others such as David Julius (Sporting Lisbon), Darius Dlhomo (Heracles), Albert 'Hurry Hurry' Johansen (Leeds) and Joseph 'Carlton' Moloi (Cardiff City) followed in Mokone's footsteps.[97]

Today every PSL player aims for an overseas contract and those who have made it big have done so spectacularly. Lucas 'Rhoo' Radebe joined Leeds United in 1994 following a record transfer deal at the time for Chiefs, his South African team, which amounted to R3,5 million. Phil Masinga of Mamelodi Sundowns also transferred to Leeds that year.

More recent players who have struck it rich include Quinton Fortune, Shaun Bartlett, Steven Pienaar and Delron Buckley. There is of course also Benni McCarthy, who emerged from the poverty of the gang-ridden Coloured townships of Cape Town to land earnings beyond even his own imagination: the estimated collective transfer fees for his moves from Cape Town to Ajax Amsterdam, Celta Vigo, Porto and eventually Blackburn Rovers total more than R190 million. His current market value has been estimated at about £7,1 million (approximately R92 million).[98]

Who would have thought that 50 years after the decision to turn the South African amateur game professional it would feature under the top ten leagues in the world in terms of revenue? With sponsorship value in the 2008–09 season at a staggering R230 million, it seems that today, more than ever, it pays to play.

8

Bucs, Birds and Amakhosi

Three of the best known – and perhaps most loved – South African soccer teams rose from the dusty streets of the Johannesburg townships. The stories of the beginnings of Orlando Pirates, Moroka Swallows and Kaizer Chiefs add vibrant colour to the decidedly black-and-white picture of yesteryear's game.

Soccer's reputation as the people's game can hardly be described better than by the history of Orlando Pirates. Pirates has had the reputation as the people's club from the outset, perhaps a reference to the background against which it was born.

It all started in Orlando, one of Soweto's biggest and most famous suburbs. In the 1930s Orlando was becoming a sprawling slum. Illegal houses built from just about anything – hessian sacks, poles, discarded sheet-iron roofing salvaged from dumpsites – mushroomed as the migration of blacks to the urban centres led to overcrowded conditions.

One of the most influential Orlando community leaders was James 'Sofasonke' Mpanza. He was a convicted murderer, but was given a reprieve at the last minute and released after he served a sentence. Having converted to Christianity while on death row, he saw himself as a kind of Moses, destined to lead his people from the bondage of homelessness and poverty.

Mpanza, who founded the Sofasonke Party in 1935, encouraged people to erect their houses on an open field in Orlando, despite not having permission from the city council. His defiance of government regulations earned him the nickname 'Sofasonke', meaning 'we will die together'.[99]

The proliferating town of tents and tumbling, makeshift structures became Mpanza's empire, which he toured on horseback and ruled with an iron fist. He was a charismatic leader who was able to move people with his hoarse, high-pitched voice, and his powerful influence spread throughout the Reef. Concerned, the city council resolved to deport him to Natal – as they did with many men with whom the township superintendents clashed – because they claimed that he was a reprobate. The intervention of his lawyers, however, thwarted this effort.

Mpanza did not tolerate crime in his kingdom. He set up what came to be known as *makgotla*, a form of people's court over which he presided and where he even dished out the punishment – lashes over the back with a rubber sjambok – personally. Outsiders often saw this punishment as being brutal, but to the people of the shanty town it was what the criminals deserved. Suspected criminals would be dragged to the 'court' screaming, and justice was dispensed swiftly. As a result, the criminals knew what their fate would be if caught and were mostly driven out of the Mpanza jurisdiction. He always said that his Christian mission and social commitment were not fully understood by his critics.

Well into his eighties, Mpanza often used to turn up at the offices of the *World* to query an article we ran about him or people from the area under his control. As far as he was concerned, they were 'his people' and he possesively protected them. Mike Ndlazi, a reporter on the *World*, was once hauled onto the bench to be whipped because of an article he had written about *makgotla*. He was given a reprieve, and warned off by Mpanza himself.

A traumatised Ndlazi returned to the office, vowing never to write anything about Mpanza again. The rule of the 'old man' had prevailed.

As Mpanza's Orlando empire grew, more and more residents started to participate in his community programmes. One of these was the Orlando Boys Club, which provided facilities for various sports, including soccer, boxing and table tennis. The associated soccer team, Orlando Boys Club FC, was founded in 1937.

The young team soon started to compete in a minor division of the JBFA. Following a dispute over what had happened to funds collected to buy soccer outfits, the team broke away from the Boys Club in 1939 and turned to Andries 'Pele Pele' Mkhwanazi for leadership. As an accomplished boxer, he was in charge of the gym at the club and well respected by the young boys. Pele Pele was reputedly the first to call them 'amapirates', possibly inspired by the adventurous endeavours of pirates depicted in films so popular at the time. [100] Under his guidance, the breakaway team rapidly progressed through the second league division of the JBFA.

The talented team, featuring greats such as Sam 'Baboon Shepherd' Shabangu, Willard 'Uyindoda' Msomi and Elliot 'Buick' Buthelezi, soon caught the eye of Bethuel Mokgosinyana, a well-respected philanthropist in Orlando. Still without official kit, Pirates received their first set of jerseys – black shirts with white sleeves and collars – from Mokgosinyana, who had dug deep into his own pocket when he originally bought the jerseys for another team. Mokgosinyana later became the patron of Orlando Pirates and the carpenter's shack behind his house in Orlando soon became known as Pirates' clubhouse. The mighty Buccaneers were set to become one of the biggest names in South African soccer.

In the 1940s Mokgosinyana sought the intervention of Mpanza when the hessian fence, which the team erected around the Donaldson Orlando Community Centre (DOCC) grounds before every game in order to charge entry fee, proved inadequate. Mpanza regarded the protest of the club as a personal crusade and demanded that the municipality should release all the grounds in Orlando for use by all the township clubs. The Bucs soon became known as '*Ezimnyama ze ka Magebula*' (Magebula's black ones) because Mpanza was informally also known in the Orlando community as Magebula (sod turner).

By the early 1950s Pirates had built up a reputation for being a stylish outfit. Fans found their elegant, clever play simply irresistible and they drew big crowds to their games. By this time Pirates had traded the JBFA-controlled facilities in favour of those managed by JAFA. This was the beginning of a hot-and-cold relationship between Pirates and the Bantu soccer structures such as the JBFA and later also SABFA. For many years Bucs opted to remain neutral, rather playing gate-taking friendly matches against various invitation sides across the country.

Following Morolo's intervention to stop the friendly game between Pirates and Highlands Park in Swaziland in 1969, a scorned SABFA enlisted the government to attack the soft belly of Pirates: the racial composition of the team. The action was aimed at Bucs goalie Gerard van der Haer, fullbacks Hans Moses and Ralph Hendricks, and strikers Rashid 'Dynamite' Khan and Bernard 'Dancing Shoes' Hartze – all Coloured and Indian players. SABFA instigated the government to ban these players from inclusion in black teams in terms of the Group Areas Act.

With such star players purged, Pirates plunged to their worst state in years, having to rebuild what had once been a mighty playing machine. In a frenzied recruiting spree they brought in mostly Pretoria players such as Conti Kekana, who later also captained the side, David 'Republic' Fakude, Duff Mogololoe, Dingaan Mokone and goalkeeper Msongela Mathebula to prop up the team. It was ironic that a group of players from Pretoria, Morolo's home town, saved Pirates in the end. Sonnyboy Ngobeni, a staunch Bucs supporter who also had his own team in Mabopane, brought in Elias 'Shuffle the Pack' Mokopane.

It was during these uncertain times that a young Irvin Khoza sneaked onto the Pirates scene. His name was to become synonymous with Orlando Pirates, following in the steps of other Orlando legends such as Mokgosinyana.

Khoza grew up in Alexandra, the bubbling cauldron of political and sporting activity on the Rand during the 1950s. With his uncle, Lucas Khoza, having been one of the driving forces behind the SASL, it is not surprising that Irvin became involved in soccer and resistance politics from an early age. [101] As a young man Khoza played for an Alexandra amateur team known as Lijabatho FC and later for Alexandra Blackpool.

He showed early leadership ability, which soon earned him the position of secretary of the Magwaza Division (what would today be termed a development division) of the Alexandra Football Association. Freelance journalist and referee Elias Kheswa often spoke of Khoza as great leadership talent and he was among those who predicted a promising future for Khoza, particularly referring to Khoza's ability to communicate with people at any level and his organisational skills.

Kheswa was killed in a robbery just when Khoza was on the cusp of his success.

Khoza broke into the inner circle of administration, however, when he was appointed as a cashier at a major soccer game. In those days no tickets were issued at the gate: one paid and entered. As there was nothing against which to reconcile gate-takings, only a trusted person could be allowed to man the ticket booth; it was not a job for just anyone. He steadily worked himself through the ranks and those who remember him from the days when he wore blue overalls while collecting money at the gates during Bucs games, can only marvel at the man who has now become probably the most influential man in South African soccer.

Although Khoza reputedly made his fortunes from property deals, soccer allowed him to flourish as an exceptional entrepreneur and leader. During the early 1980s he briefly held the position of Pirates' secretary and returned about a decade later to take over an almost bankrupt, ailing Pirates and build it into the empire that it is today.

His return to the administration ranks of Pirates followed a resolution by the influential Committee of Seven, a group of staunch female supporters who made sure their voice was heard at Pirates meetings. Bucs meetings were, for all intents and purposes, meetings of the Orlando community. Fans would pack the DOCC at these meetings and have a say as to which officials had to be elected or fired.

Khoza therefore faced much opposition when he took over the leadership at Pirates, especially since the idea of one person having control over Bucs – 'the people's club' – was unfathomable. The Orlando community were particularly sensitive to such an appointment, as it would mean a loss of control over what they perceived to be their community asset. But Khoza insists that his intervention was meant to save Bucs from those who wanted to register the club as a private company without keeping the interests of the community at heart.

His life has not been without drama and event, however. He has had many encounters with the law, which an international media report about him played up to question South Africa's ability to host a successful World Cup tournament.[102] His power has spread to both the PSL, which he rules as chairman, and SAFA.

Khoza's power of persuasion is legendary. Being boss of Pirates is not an easy job. Fans demand immediate and ongoing success, and players have often had to face the supporters' wrath when they did not deliver. Former coach, Gordon Ingesund, was once attacked at a training session after Pirates had lost a few games – despite having won the league championship the previous year.

But Khoza can face up to these challenges. He emphasises that he does not have a bodyguard, drives his own car and lives among his people in Soweto. His presence intimidates, and whispers about him are silenced when he appears. He is combative and robust when the need arises, and the world of soccer, generally made up of plotters and cliques, quivers when he speaks.

Yet, deep down, Khoza is a gentle family man. When his daughter died of an AIDS-related disease, he was devastated but had the courage to come out and talk about it; when his team won the 1995 Africa Champions Cup in the sweltering heat in Abidjan, Ivory Coast against all odds, he shed a tear in the hotel room after the game. His boys had achieved what had been thought an impossible mission. And he added a prayer in thanks.

The manner in which he went about to rebuild Bucs is typical of his style. He had a vision, not only for Pirates but also for soccer generally.

When Jomo Sono's team, Cosmos, were relegated from the NPSL in 1989, Khoza approached the legendary former Pirates player to negotiate transferring some of his players to Bucs – a master stroke. Khoza knew that deep inside, Sono still felt an affinity for Pirates, the team that his father had so capably led and that later gave him his break into professional soccer. This expedition yielded players such as Mark Fish, Helman Mkhelelele and Linda 'Mercedes' Buthelezi – all of whom went on to play internationally – who joined John Moeti, Innocent Mncwango, Brendon Silent and Nick 'Bazooka' Sishweni to create one of the more exciting sides Bucs have had. Indeed, this was to form the basis of the side that won the Africa Champions Cup a few years later – the only Southern African team to achieve this honour.

Khoza's vision also included ensuring that Pirates obtained a home stadium over which they had control. Fertiliser and beer magnate Louis Luyt, then at the helm of the Transvaal Rugby Union, had signed a long lease on the 60,000-seat Ellis Park Stadium from the Johannesburg City Council. The Union had demolished the old stadium and built a new, modern facility of R53 million. With an uncanny ability to seize opportunities, Khoza developed a relationship with the management committee of the Golden Lions.

In 2005 a joint venture was set up between a company called Interza Lesego, Pirates and Ellis Park (Pty) Ltd, with Bucs owning 51% of the company. This technically means that Bucs is the only team that effectively owns their home ground, now known as Coca-Cola Park.

The Iron Duke indeed holds his Pirates in an iron grip. It is he who takes the final decision on player signings. It is he who negotiates contracts. And it is he who decides whether a player, once a Pirate, is always a Pirate.

Ten years after the birth of Pirates, a flock of Swallows announced their arrival to create the basis for a fierce rivalry on the Soweto soccer scene, perhaps one of the biggest on the continent.

The Birds – Moroka Swallows – made their nest in Moroka and its neighbouring townships in the central area of Soweto. The township, like many other black settlements, was known as 'Masakeng' (hessian sacks). It was typical of the shanty towns that dotted the landscape of what is now known as Soweto. In the streets, young boys who erected makeshift poles on a patch on the road reasonably free from the dirty water, and sometimes raw sewage flow, spiritedly played their game.

'Everywhere we looked, we saw a barefoot boy juggling with a tennis ball or playing in a game on the streets,' one of the founders, Strike Makgatho, says in an interview on the club's website.[103] Many talented young players were identified, taken off the streets and introduced to formal soccer. It took almost seven years of hard work by three soccer enthusiasts, Ishmael Lesolang, Makgatho and Johnny Kubheka, to get Swallows, formally established in 1947, to soar.

By 1953 some players from Swallows technically played for two teams – one a team representing workers at Amalgamated Packaging, for whom they played on Saturdays, and the other Swallows, whose games were played on Sundays.

The team achieved great success during the 1950s and '60s, including winning the league championship of the SASL. The Birds won the Transvaal Challenge in 1956 and the Robinson Cup in 1958 and 1959.

The Birds claim to have been the first to establish an official supporters club. Their fans are still as passionate now as they were in the early years, when they would flap their arms in the air and shout 'don't follow me, follow the Birds!' The fans were often just as volatile as officials such as Elijah 'Boy Baarde' Nhlapo. Nhlapo, who was unhappy over an article that I had written, once mistakenly attacked my colleague, Elliot Makhaya, at a match at the Moroka Jabavu Stadium. At the same time a flock of birds flew over the stadium and the fans cheered madly, which Nhlapo believed was support and endorsement for his actions. Makhaya had to be escorted out of the stadium.

For just more than a decade Swallows were a formidable team. Not even the absence of their mainstay and striker Joseph 'Carlton' Moloi, who left the team in 1959 to join Welsh club Cardiff City, could affect the performance of the team. Swallows were the first Johannesburg team to sign up for the SASL.

But during the sixites the team went through turbulent times. This ranged from having to deal with their star players being kidnapped ahead of major games – something that happened quite regularly in soccer, particularly when supporters placed bets on the outcome of the game – to several splits that resulted in assaults and even the death of players.

Such splits weakened the team considerably. Various versions of Swallows emerged. First, there was Swallows, but after a split over affiliation, Moroka Swallows (Mbanya) or Swallows Babes, was formed and led by Differ Mbanya. Then followed Real Moroka Swallows and Moroka Swallows Big XV. Four star players left Swallows to form Mighty Birds – a tragic move in which one of them was shot and killed. Finally, David 'Pine' Chabeli led a group who registered the name Moroka Swallows Limited as a company, which is the current Moroka Swallows that features in the Premiership.

Swallows toughie 'Boy Baarde' Nhlapo once summoned the

taxi drivers outside Dube Station in Soweto to attack a team of *World* journalists because of an article about one version of Swallows. Our lives were saved by businessman Baba Nkosi who locked us in his shop across the road from the station.

Those were violent times at Moroka Swallows. It required the intervention of Jack 'Big Daddy' Sello to bring stability to the Birds after almost a decade of internal strife. Together with Sylvester Masinga, Abe Machele, 'Boy Baarde' Nhlapo, and David Chabeli, he began to rebuild the Birds. The process, which entailed building team morale, improving internal management structures and Chabeli, one of the best talent scouts, finding new players, culminated in the Swallows team as we know it today.

A significant event in South African club football occurred in an unexpected place.

One morning in early 1970, Ewert 'The Lip' Nene, Thomas 'Zero My Hero' Johnson, Ratha 'Greaves' Mokgoatlheng and Edward 'Msomi' Khoza walked into the offices of the *World*, sporting an assortment of injuries. We had heard that there had been drama at a general meeting of Orlando Pirates at the DOCC the previous night and that several players and an official had been assaulted for having played for a team in Botswana without permission.

As the four recounted the story, a picture of an emotionally charged meeting unfolded. Perhaps true to their 'people's team' credo, fans made binding decisions about the team and even elected officials to run the club. The eventful meeting, scheduled to be just a regular meeting of Bucs supporters, was due to start, but officials had not turned up yet. Impatiently, the fans called for Salthiel Chochoe to start the meeting. He was cheered on with shouts of 'Black Power!' – a phrase reflecting his involvement in political activism and which fans often used to cheer him on during games.

The meeting took its usual format, until the matter of players taking part in 'unauthorised' games came up. It was not unusual for players to keep themselves busy during the Christmas recess by guest-playing in friendly games, usually in their home towns. However, many teams discouraged this practice as they had no control over who played for whom, and against whom. For example, Pimville United Brothers' dashing left-winger Sidney 'Skheshekheshe' Sebiloane's budding career was prematurely ended when he broke his leg in a reckless tackle during one such game.

Over the 1969 Christmas recess, some Pirates players engaged in guest appearances for other clubs: Percy 'Chippa' Moloi in Swaziland, and Johnson, Mokgoatlheng and Khoza in Botswana. The latter had been invited by Johnson's friend to guest for his team, as an attraction for the fans. But the players had not sought Pirates' permission to play in those games.

Led by the vociferous Moipone Moorosi, a tough and feared member of the Committee of Seven, the Bucs supporters accused the players, and also Allen 'Chain Puller' Chiyi who was meant to join the guys in Botswana, of gross insubordination. When club manager Nene tried to defend them, he was attacked and all hell broke loose. They had to flee for their lives.

Bruised and upset, Nene and his group wanted to know why similar action had not been taken against Percy Moloi, who had not only played as a guest, but also coached a team in Swaziland over the same period. The story made front page news in that afternoon's edition of *World*.

With deadlines gone, the four chatted to us about their future and we were joined in the sports department by sub-editor Cyril McAravey. Sports editor Leslie Sehume asked the players whether they would be able to go back to Orlando Pirates, but they all agreed it would be impossible, as they had been expelled. McAravey then asked them about their relationship with former Pirates player Kaizer Motaung, who was playing for Atlanta Chiefs in the United States at the time and was due to return to South Africa during the season break. He suggested that Motaung be persuaded to join them in playing as an Invitation XI, and the idea excited Nene in particular.

A telephone call to Motaung was promptly made from our offices. Understandably, Motaung was quite wary of what might happen to him and his family were he to leave Pirates, but he was positive nonetheless and agreed to explore the matter. McAravey called Sundowns striker Ingle Singh, who was just as excited at the prospect of participating in such an Invitation XI. He in turn brought fellow Pretoria players Roy Fischer and goalkeeper Vincent 'Tanti' Julius on board. On Motaung's arrival back in the country, the final details were fixed and the Kaizer XI were set up. Their exploratory game against an Invitation XI was scheduled for the Newlands Stadium in the Coloured township Newclare, west of Johannesburg – thanks to Henry Ritson, a sports organiser in the township who ensured that the venue was available.

Much organisation had to be done before the first boot could be put to ball. Soccer jerseys and socks had to be organised, and the important decision about team colours had to be made. McAravey went out seeking sponsored outfits or a donation of outfits. In the end, he was offered a set of jerseys – and they just happened to be the yellow and black that the team, which eventually became Kaizer Chiefs, still wear today. Chiefs now suggest that the specific colours were chosen as they were the same as those of the English team Wolverhampton Wanderers.

The success of the new team was immediate and matches

were arranged in several centres. The role of the *World* was significant, largely because it was in the interest of the newspaper to create soccer competition in order to boost its sales. The *World*'s offices were the meeting place of officials from soccer clubs – amateur and professional – and as there was no structured fixture programme most of the time, friendly game deals were often struck there. Soccer activities made front page news, helping the clubs to grow their supporter base.

It was clear that in order to succeed, clubs needed the support of the newspaper, and the *World*'s support to the Kaizer XI was largely responsible for the initial success of the team. Individual journalists also played a role, for example, Benoni-based journalist-cum-priest Maziph Mtshali who helped to organise match venues on the East Rand for the new team, while colleague Elliot Makhaya organised the Thokoza soccer officials to support friendly matches for the Kaizer XI at the Thokoza Stadium. Makhaya went even further: as music reporter, he enlisted the services of music mogul Rupert Bopape to help raise operational funds for the Kaizer XI in exchange for publicity for his musicians Simon 'Mahlathini' Nkabinde and the Mahotella Queens in the newspaper.

McAravey is of the opinion that the success of the Kaizer Invitation team at its inception would not have been achieved without the enthusiastic support they received from smaller teams. Witbank Black Aces patron, Jabu Khumalo, and legendary manager Sy Mtimunye put their weight behind the campaign and loaned players such as Slow Masuku, Donald Mashabela and Ace Mkhonza to the Kaizer XI. Atteridgeville's Spa Sporting Club also offered the services of Russa 'Uncle' Bud-Mbele and their youthful midfield maestro, Arial 'Pro' Kgongoane, to the new team. Kgongoane later captained the first black African national team.

McAravey played a prominent role in managing the process of establishing the Kaizer XI. His late night forays into Soweto – without the special permit whites needed to enter the black township – were to meet with players and officials from various associations in an effort to ensure the new team got off the ground. 'Many times we would note an unmarked Special Branch police car following us, and we would play games by taking quick turns into alleys to lose the tail. But the frightening thing is that there were times when I did not see them. They would call the general manager at the *World* to tell him that they had seen me the night before and that I was "playing with fire" by spending all this time in Soweto,' he recalls, laughing.

Bethuel Morolo's SABFA closed the door on the new team, stating that associations affiliated to his organisation – therefore those that had access to playing grounds – should not accommodate the team. But money lured, and many associations saw an invitation to host the team as an opportunity to make a quick rand or two.

The talent-identifying skills of Ewert Nene came in particularly handy when it came to recruiting players for the new team. During the invitation games several new talented players were approached to sign up with the Kaizer XI, which is how Ariel 'Pro' Kgongoane from Spa Sporting Club, and Ace Ntsoelengoe and Banks Setlhodi from the Randfontein Invitation XI joined the team.

McAravey recalls organising a match for the Kaizer XI in the then South West Africa (Namibia). A charter plane was arranged to fly the team to Windhoek, and says McAravey: 'If the truth be told, we did not have money to pay for the charter flight, but we gave them a cheque with the hope that we would have collected enough to pay in before they deposited the cheque.'

The team returned home with new recruit Herman 'Pele' Blaschke, but without the expected money as the gate-takings were lower than anticipated. When the flight was delayed owing to a technical problem, McAravey made up a story and argued with the charter company to reduce the cost because, he claimed, they had missed a game in Johannesburg, and therefore income.

Another Namibian player, Pius Eigowab, followed later and a game against a Natal Invitation XI yielded Bomber Chamane and Abednigo 'Shaka' Ngcobo.

By 1971, the time had arrived for Motaung to decide whether the Kaizer XI would become a permanent team. At that time the local soccer scene was a predictable Pirates–Swallows affair, and Motaung suggests that his father convinced him that it would be in the interest of South African soccer if another team was formed. Pirates also seemed resistant to some of the changes that he had proposed after his experience in the United States. [104] This helped him to make up his mind, as he was convinced that such changes – relating to management style and tactical and technical awareness – were in the interest of soccer in South Africa.

The team had to have a name, of course, and it was decided to append Chiefs – from Kaizer's American team, the Atlanta Chiefs – to their leader's name. It was an apt choice indeed, as chiefs are important figures in the traditional black African culture: they are the wise, powerful leaders of the community, and they rule supreme.

Kaizer Chiefs was formally structured in January 1971, with Motaung, 'China' Ngema, Clarence Mlokoti, Gilbert Sekgabi and Ewert Nene at the helm. In response to the threats of violence from angry Bucs supporters, Nene used the 'Love and Peace' slogan, popularised by the 'hippies' of the time, to neutralise the anger. He insisted on making the 'V' sign when-ever a photograph was taken of him and actually demanded a photograph every time he came into the offices of *World* – sometimes twice or three times a week!

As Chiefs was not affiliated to any association at that time, the JBFA refused to recommend them to the NPSL. JBFA secretary Ephraim Tshabalala demanded that, like any other team, they should work their way through the ranks to be recommended for NPSL membership, because none of the teams affiliated to the JBFA would agree to Chiefs being pushed through ahead of them.

However, Matthew Mpahane, a streetwise administrator and president of the Nigel Football Association, invited Chiefs to join his association. The new team was promptly recommended to the NPSL, overcoming the constitutional obstacle the NPSL had raised regarding Chiefs' affiliation. The truth, however, is that the NPSL needed Chiefs desperately, and Mpahane was able to horse-trade on this transaction. The payback, Mpahane told me at the time, was that his own team, Nigel United Buccaneers, had to be promoted from the First Division to the NPSL the following season, and he would hold the officials of the league to it. This meant Nigel Buccaneers had to top the log at the end of the season and, so the story goes, it was arranged that the majority of the Nigel team's first-round league fixtures would be home games.

There were even suggestions that 'sympathetic' referees were appointed to handle the games, and by the end of the first round Nigel Buccaneers were comfortably top of the log. That achieved, it was resolved that there would not be a second round and Nigel Buccaneers – led by Rhyder Nhlangothi – were promoted to the NPSL! Papius Zwane's Mamelodi United had to pay the price and were relegated to accommodate the

Nigel side. It was clear, however, that the Nigel team would be out of their league, so to speak, but Mpahane consoled himself by pointing out that other teams, like Dalton Brothers, who were no better, also competed in the league. A season in the top flight would have generated substantial enough income to allow Mpahane to run the team if they were relegated.

Pirates, Chiefs and Swallows are today still the prime teams in the Premier League of the NSL, even though many teams have caught up with them in terms of performance. Hearing enthusiastic cheers of the fans, there is little doubt about the impression Bucs, Birds and Amakhosi have made on the South African soccer scene.

9

The gods of football

Weekends in Soweto – and other black townships – were fairly predictable during the 1970s. The days were set aside for socially important matters: weddings, funerals, *stokvels*.[105] And soccer.

Without access to television, soccer fans were glued to their battery-operated portable radios, listening to commentary of critical games. On Saturday 10 February 1979, Jomo Sono also listened to the radio while sitting in his car, pondering what might have been. What was significant about this is that he had just concluded the formalities of getting married, and there was a buzz around. It was, after all, a wedding and in African tradition, a time of joyous celebration, ululations and merry-making. But Sono's mind was elsewhere.

His team, Orlando Pirates, were playing a critical game at the Rand Stadium, and were, by all accounts, in desperate trouble. They were up against the white Highlands Park and with Highlands coach Joe Frickleton's earlier comments about black teams being technically and organisationally inferior in mind, it was one of those defining moments for soccer, and black soccer in particular.

Sono's father-in-law spotted the forlorn boy and immediately knew what the problem was. The bridegroom did not need much persuasion to go to the stadium and with the permission of his father-in-law, he sped off. Like most soccer players who owned a car, Sono kept his kit in the boot, always ready for a kick-about and target shooting practise.

On his arrival at the stadium, Bucs were trailing 0–2, and their supporters were stunned into silence. Enter Sono. It took only one fan to demand he get onto the pitch. Sono was soon in his kit and onto the field; his colleagues offered to make way. In those days it was possible for a player to just arrive and be drafted into the team, even without his name being on the original team sheet. Once on the field, Sono soon scored two goals and created two more. Bucs won the game 4–2! Mission accomplished, he went back to the business of the wedding.

Even after so many years, Sono still enjoys recounting this story in interviews; fans no doubt enjoy reminiscing about the Sono impact.

South African soccer fans first became aware of the talented young Sono during a friendly match between Orlando Pirates and Ga-Rankuwa Kilmarnock in 1971.[106] On the dusty patch alongside the railway line, which local side Kilmarnock used as their home ground, the game provided an opportunity for Bucs to test their new player in a competitive situation. Kilmarnock were no walk-over side, as many teams will attest, and their home ground was often referred to as their 'slaughter-house'.

Ephraim Sono, who later became popularly known as Jomo,[107] played a blinder. As journalists, we did not need official team lists at the time; we knew all the players. But the talented new player was an unfamiliar face. When I approached Bucs officials during the game to enquire, their praise knew no end. Later, Sir Stanley Matthews, who briefly played in South

Africa and conducted soccer clinics in the black townships, enthused over Sono, predicting a great future for him.

Sono soon became one of the game's icons, just like his father, the legendary Pirates captain Eric 'Scara' Sono. The array of names he was called by reflects his impact on South African soccer: Black Prince, King of African soccer, Troublemaker, Kop (meaning 'head' in Afrikaans), Scara, Heartbreaker. The name 'Banana boy' comes from his trademark curving kick, also known as the banana kick, which he practised with hoops fixed to the corners of goalposts. Today the players at Cosmos respectfully call him 'Bra J' or 'Big J'.

By 1974 he had had a stint with Sporting Lisbon in Portugal and had received various honours, including sharing the field with legends like Pele, George Best, Carlos Alberto Parreira, Ray Clemens and Kevin Keegan in a World XI in Japan, and also playing for Toronto Blizzards and New York Cosmos. The team he played for in the Big Apple served as inspiration when he had to choose a name for his own team – Jomo Cosmos – more than two decades later. Other players had done the same with their teams, for example, Kaizer Motaung with the Chiefs, Percy 'Chippa' Moloi with Chippa Stars and Ace Ntsoelengoe with Ace Kicks.

Another star player of the mid-1970s and 1980s was Patrick 'Ace' Ntsoelengoe, who was considered the best midfielder of his generation. Radio commentator Dan Setshedi nicknamed him 'Mabheka Phantsi' (he who looks down), because he deceptively seemed to look down on the ball as he strolled forward – he was a master of slowing down the game – before taking off with blinding brilliance and creating space for his strikers to score.

His impressive talent earned him a place in Kaizer Chiefs, where he arguably became one of the most respected South

African soccer players. 'Oom Dan', as Setshedi was known, enthused over this talent. 'It's so sad that we don't play international soccer. This boy would have led a South African team any time,' he told me once as we drove back from the stadium after covering a Chiefs game.

Ntsoelengoe was discovered while playing for the Randfontein Invitation XI against the Kaizer XI. I covered the game for the *World* and with Ewert Nene sitting on a bench next to me, I was privy to his thoughts about all the players in the Randfontein team. In a moment of sheer brilliance, Ntsoelengoe burst past the shaky Kaizer XI – enough to convince Nene of his talent.

Nene smiled. 'I am taking that boy with us today,' he told me. 'And that one too,' he added, referring to Joseph 'Banks' Setlhodi, the Randfontein goalkeeper, who had then just made a brilliant dive to stop a goal from Kaizer Motaung.

It was the beginning of a career that eventually took Ace Ntsoelengoe to the United States to play in the North American Soccer League – thanks to Motaung's contacts. He played in North America for eleven seasons – more than any other South African player – featuring for teams such as Minnesota Kicks, Denver Dynamos and Toronto Blizzards.

But despite the many great soccer players South Africa has produced over the years, my vote for one of the best goes to Lucas 'Masterpieces' Moripe.

Back in 1970, Elliot Makhaya had written a feature on Moripe for the sports pages of the *World* in which he described him as a 'miracle'. He used such superlatives that sports editor Leslie Sehume and I dismissed Makhaya's article for being too full of hyperbole. The article was spiked – much to Makhaya's chagrin. He was so convinced of Moripe's talent that he challenged me to make time to watch the young man in action. Moripe's team, Pretoria Callies (then known as Bantu Callies), had a game against Rangers FC from Eersterust at the old Phelindaba Stadium coming up.

It is not an exaggeration to say that waves and waves of soccer fans made their way to the stadium by about 15:00 that afternoon. Shebeens rapidly emptied and Ada – as Moripe's local supporters called him – was the sole subject of animated discussion along the streets leading to the stadium. People jostled for space and when the game kicked off, a massive roar went up.

However, it was nothing compared to the cheer when Moripe made his first touch. He did not disappoint. It was almost as if my colleague Makhaya had told him beforehand that we would be watching and he was putting on a display. But it turned out that that was just how he played his game. Brilliant on the ball, a master of deception, and one of the best passers of the ball I have seen – and I have seen many before, and since.

The game ended and the fans made their way back to the shebeens where discussions about Moripe continued. We went to one such shebeen with Makhaya, and I could sense the buzz that Moripe had generated. Each fan recalled a specific moment of the game – not so much the goals, but how Moripe had created moves. Callies had won, but that was secondary. Moripe had given another display and the fans were already looking forward to the next weekend's game.

Needless to say, the feature was published and even sceptical soccer fans outside of Pretoria seemed to wait for the moment to see this player. Moripe was on every soccer fan's lips.

'I just loved making the ball talk to me,' Moripe said when I asked him about his playing days.[108] It was indeed as if he could almost make the ball do anything he wanted.

Moripe joined Callies from Huns Sporting Club, where he had been nurtured by brothers Melvin and Joey Mokone, who spotted his talent early on. The story goes that he and a playing partner at Huns' second division once dribbled their way past the midfield and defence of the opposition to draw out the goalkeeper, who they also dribbled past. Instead of scoring, they reputedly turned back on the goal line and challenged each other to do it all over again. It was this kind of 'street football' that kept him in the junior division for a long time.

Friends at Callies recognised that his talent would complement the typical hard-running, striking play of Phillip 'Chesa' Sibanda and Gideon 'Score' Varrie.

In 1973, a team consisting of British professional soccer stars, mostly in the twilight of their careers, arrived in South Africa The British All Stars XI, led by Rodney Marsh, played against a team of players from NPSL clubs at the Orlando Stadium. Moripe came on as substitute, but soon captured the imagination of thousands of spectators when he ran all the way from the centre line to score a goal for the NPSL XI, leaving British players sprawled – literally – in his wake. It was legendary.

'It was a game I will never forget,' Moripe recalls. 'I had felt that I was somehow being starved of the ball, and decided that from wherever I got the ball, I would make a solo effort to score. Kaizer Motaung received the ball from the back, and found me along the centre line on the right. I decided to take on all comers – and I left them all sprawling, including the goalkeeper!' he beams during an interview at his modest Atteridgeville home. [109]

The game proved to be the turning point in his career. He not only won the Sportsman of the Year Award, but was also made an offer to play in Hong Kong where he had a short spell with Caroline Hills. But after just a few games he became so homesick that he asked to be released and returned to South Africa.

Moripe built up a legion of fans, admirers and supporters. If the truth be told, had he been born in Johannesburg and in his prime played for one of the big teams of the time – Orlando Pirates, Kaizer Chiefs or Moroka Swallows – he would have been acknowledged even more. In fact, he was soon nicknamed 'Soweto' and declared their own by Soweto soccer fans. Elsewhere, he was dubbed 'Modimo wa Bolo' (the god of soccer).

Once, when Callies was fixtured to play against Moroka Swallows in a midweek night game at Orlando Stadium, the *World* reported that Moripe was injured. Our phones rang off the hook that day, with fans declaring that if Moripe was not going to play it would not be worth going to the match. They demanded that Callies coach Dick Phiri field him, saying that a half-fit Moripe was worth any two players Callies could field. Later, hundreds of fans waited outside the stadium for kick-off – and assurance that Moripe was on the field before they paid their entry fee.

Another Callies coach, John 'Mochacho' Georgiadis, built Callies into a strong defensive team and he often had conflicts with Moripe over his style. I sat in during one interval team talk, which in those days took place right on the pitch, and listened to Georgiadis reprimanding the players for not following his instructions. In his animated Greek English he reproached them one by one:

'Patrick [Dibeṭla], why you leave the ball and kick the man? Why? Why?'

'Frank ['Mahazel' Ramashala], I tell you not to leave your man alone, but you leave him. Why? Why?'

'Patrick ['LTD' Molala], why you take the ball and run away

from the goals? You go to the corner, and you lose the ball. Why? Why?'

Exasperated, he turned to Moripe. 'Lucas, you take the ball, the people they say "Master!". You dribble, you dribble; the people they say "Master!". You lose the ball, the people they say "sorry". We lose the game, the people they say "Mochacho"! Why, why, why?'

But the kind of disciplined, one-touch football that John Georgiadis demanded from Moripe simply was not his style. He was skilful and knew how to open up defences, and it was when Callies were under real pressure that his skills were seen.

Once asked how he executed dribbling moves, Moripe said that it happened so fast, and naturally, that he could not remember what he had done. There was no television and he could not watch replays. Those movements are gone forever – lost in the mist of time.

A training stint in England exposed Moripe to the rigours of English football, specfically while training with West Ham United and Wolverhampton. 'I learnt a lot there. Their game is more direct, but a player like Sir Stanley Matthews was pretty much the kind of player I was – taking on defences, creating space for your teammates and letting them score,' he says.

Those who have played with Moripe on the same team echo his words, convinced it was his brilliance that allowed them to shine; opponents dreaded him. Indeed, his play inspired many wins for Callies. During one such memorable match against Orlando Pirates at the Atteridgeville Super Stadium, Moripe played a brilliant game, bamboozling the Bucs defence to see Callies lead 2–1. The Bucs fans could not take it and goalkeeper Patson 'Kamazu' Banda could be heard shouting, in vain, at his defence to stop the marauding Moripe. Banda later claimed that he had been hit by a brick from angry fans. The game was abandoned when the fans rioted. Callies won the replay by the same margin, Moripe again inspiring the victory.

Moripe had a brief, but unhappy, stint with Orlando Pirates. He believes that he was deliberately starved of the ball and therefore could not play to his best. Many, however, believe that he joined Pirates in the twilight of his sparkling career.

Moripe suffered a stroke and was wheelchair-bound for more than five years. Following a rehabilitation programme he is able to walk again, albeit supported by crutches. He still attracts salutes from fans who remember the good times that he provided for them on the field. Is there another Moripe on the horizon? Soccer analysts doubt it. Many have been compared to Moripe, but it turned out to be deceptively flattering comparisons. Yet it is not inconceivable that another talent lurks in the township streets, waiting to be discovered.

There are many other stars whose unique style added lustre to yesteryear's game. One such player is the audacious former centre-forward for Avalon Athletics, Dharam Mohan. He is remembered for his strength, his shooting skills and uncanny ability to shield the ball. Mohan made his debut in professional soccer at the famed Curries Fountain ground in Durban in 1958 and later also captained the great Avalon side of the 1960s. He played professionally until 1966, when his career was brought to a grinding halt because the apartheid government sounded the death knell for the SASL.

Mohan can probably pass as the best striker of the ball the country has had, although it is open to debate. He played in a different time: the styles were different and, some would argue, the game was not as tactically developed – for better or worse – as it is now. Mohan played with, and against, the likes of Eric 'Scara' Sono, Conrad Stuurman, Kaizer 'King Kaizer

Matatazela' Mkhwanazi, the legendary Cedric 'Sugar Ray' Xulu and a host of other prominent SASL players.

Bernard 'Dancing Shoes' Hartze also deserves mention in this group, not least for his record goal-scoring average in the FPL. Shoes originally played for Pretoria team Sundowns – led by Ingle Singh – at the famous Muslim Grounds in Marabastad, west of the city. In reality it was just a patch of open ground, which you reached down a footpath. Paying 25 cents admission fee at a table a hundred metres or so away from the ground, spectators could watch the home team against the likes of Orlando Pirates, Moroka Swallows and Kliptown Burnley. Fans came in their thousands – travelling from Atteridgeville, Ga-Rankuwa and Mamelodi – to watch the brilliant Shoes in action. They called him 'Bernard the Best'.

He later joined Orlando Pirates, but his Buccaneer days abruptly ended when SABFA banned him and other 'Coloured' players from playing for a black African team. He also had short stints in the United States, where he played for Tampa Bay Rowdies. He finally settled in Cape Town where he played for Cape Town Spurs, Cape Town City and Hellenic. He still holds the record for the most goals scored in a league season, namely 35 in 16 matches.[110]

For sheer dribbling skill, however, there was Joel 'Ace' Mnini, the Moroka Swallows left-winger who created havoc among defences when in full flight. He often single-handedly prised open defences to allow the raw striking force of Swallows – Andries 'Six Mabone' Maseko and Congo Malebane – to score crucial goals. It was the manner of his play, directly taking on defenders who would be on the retreat as the crowds shouted approval, that made him such a marvel to watch. He was seldom wasteful in his dribbling, which also set him apart from many other ball jugglers.

Mnini originally joined Swallows from an amateur side in Zola, Soweto, but quietly faded from the scene at the height of in-fighting at Swallows – one of many who decided to retire for their own safety. Many believe that his talent would have earned him great accolades had he not ended his career so early. Today Mnini coaches a development side of Moroka Swallows.

As much as the stars of South African soccer are part of the game's history, so are the distinctive playing styles that have developed in this country. South African fans enjoy the art of dribbling and the 'Diski One One' style attracts many spectators to the stadiums. Dribbling often forms part of the local game – all in an effort to break down the opposition's defence.

Cunning dribblers of the past include Swallows player Irvin 'Pepe' Dire, who took the dribbling skills of the kind demonstrated by Difference 'City Council' Mbanya to a new level, and Groovin Molope, who often feigned a pass and then defiantly asked his opponent 'Do you drink Groovy?'[111] Bantala Shigo of Pretoria Callies was known for his repertoire of dance moves, which he often combined with pretending to play a guitar, while waltzing past defenders.

Over the years many different styles have developed. 'Shibobo' – the player pushing the ball between the legs of an opponent and then rounding him – was introduced around 1998. The name of the style comes from the title of a hip-hop song by music group TKZee. The song was recorded in 1998, ahead of South Africa's first appearance at a soccer World Cup (in France) and featured star player Benni McCarthy rapping. It became an instant hit, both locally and internationally. McCarthy went on to score Bafana's first ever World Cup goal – a 'shibobo' which he slid between the legs of Denmark's goalie Peter Schmeichel.

Another style was the 'Show me your number', which involved an attacking player faking a shot, forcing the opponent to turn to protect himself from being blasted with the ball. The 'Tsamaya' style (walk) involved pushing the ball by the sole of the foot and then literally walking forward to invite the opposition to come and get the ball – if they dared. The 'V-dribble' involved playing the ball around a defender and passing him from the opposite side, thereby creating a 'V' pattern.

It is often said that South African players overdo dribbling to show off their skills, rather than putting it to positive use to win games. Lekkie Ramela's 1970s Meadowlands Giant Aces are a prime example: the players often mused over how they dribbled past their opponents, only for the listener to find out that they actually lost the game!

The lack of tactical discipline that makes dribbling wasteful is often scorned by coaches. Players like Scara Ngobese, formerly of Kaizer Chiefs, and Shakes Ngwenya of Mamelodi Sundowns, are crowd favourites because of their nifty touches, but spend the best part of the season on the bench because they are regarded as wasteful dribblers. An internationally famous player such as Sir Stanley Matthews, who was known during his playing days as 'The Wizard of the Dribble' and 'The Magician', was all the rage during his playing days. Matthews could deftly make a final pass to his striking teammates and his dribbling skills were described in a recollection of a famours incident when England took on Italy in 1948. With England leading 4–0, Matthews reportedly dribbled towards the corner flag where he stood with his boot on the ball, wiped his hands on his pants and neatly pushed his hair back while waiting for challengers to come at him. Some fans even suggested he took out a comb and combed his hair in a display of showboating, but this suggestion is most likely part of the legend that grew around Sir Stan. South African soccer fans will remember Scara Ngobese doing something similar, much to the chagrin of his coach Muhsin Ertrugal.

Johan Cruyff, Pele and more recently Ronaldo, Thierry Henry and Manchester players Cristiano Ronaldo and Ryan Giggs, however, are greatly admired for their dribbling style because they are regarded as creative rather than wasteful dribblers.

About a year before the 2010 World Cup, the Diski Dance was introduced to soccer fans in a television campaign by South African Tourism, based on the Diski One One style. According to the national tourism body, the Diski Dance is meant to give visitors the chance to feel the rhythm of African football. The advert was aired on several international sports and news channels in the run-up to the tournament. Soccer fans quickly picked up on it and were soon dancing in step.

10

'The Boys'

After decades of isolation, South Africa triumphantly returned to the international sporting arena during the early 1990s. And what a kick-off to the new era it was!

In 1995 the country erupted into wild celebration when Francois Pienaar's Springboks won the Rugby World Cup, and President Nelson Mandela was on hand to present the coveted trophy to the captain – and the nation. Later that year, Orlando Pirates won the Africa Champions Cup,[112] the first – and thus far only – Southern African club to achieve this honour. 1996 brought even more glory. South Africa's new national soccer team won the Africa Cup of Nations, and later that year Josiah Thugwane, Hezekiel Sepeng and Penny Heyns brought back a handful of medals from the Atlanta Olympics. South Africa was back!

The build-up to the soccer success of the mid-nineties began in 1992. South Africa embarked on a process of shedding its apartheid past and developing democratic structures, and CAF gave SAFA permission to stage a symbolic return-to-the-family friendly series against Cameroon. After the ignominy of being expelled from the first Africa Cup of Nations, by an organisation of which they were a founding partner, South Africa needed a massive lift to make a return to international football.

In July of that year, a truly representative side turned out for South Africa in an international soccer match for the first time. The first match took place at the Kings Park Rugby Stadium in Durban. When Botswana referee Jelas Masole and his assistants took to the field, followed by Neil Tovey and his team – Mark Anderson, David Nyathi, Lucas Radebe, Ewee Khambule, Zane Moosa, Didi Khuse, Doctor Khumalo, Fani Madida and Phil Masinga – the 40,000-strong crowd erupted into song and dance.

The Cameroon team, which included the legendary Roger Milla, threw everything at the South Africans. Coach Stanley Tshabalala, who achieved success at club level with his 'shoe-shine and piano' coaching style (playing a rhythmic one-touch game), knew that nothing short of victory would be acceptable to the fans hungry for the excitement of international football.

The game swung from end to end and it seemed to be headed for a draw. However, the introduction of Augustine 'Mthakathi' Makalakalane, wearing his trademark white soccer boots, was just the inspiration needed. His distribution into the eighteen-yard area created a pressure situation that resulted in a penalty for the home side. Doctor Khumalo swept the ball past a diving Cameroon goalkeeper a mere eight minutes before the final whistle.

The cheers from the crowd must have reverberated through the nearby black townships of Kwa Mashu, Lamontville and Umlazi; it certainly echoed across the country. South Africa had announced their return as they held on to the narrow 1–0 lead.

Two days later, the euphoria was brought to an abrupt end when the Cameroonians took on South Africa once more – this time at the Goodwood Showgrounds in Cape Town. Tshabalala fielded several new players. Steve Khompela was introduced to defence, Sizwe Motaung replaced Neil Tovey as captain and Duncan Crowie replaced the bustling Phil Masinga as striker. Two other debutants, Mark Williams and Benjamin Reed, also had a run. It was an intense game during which two Cameroon players were given red cards and another two – including Roger Milla – were cautioned. The team from West Africa was not about to be beaten a second time and an own goal by a Cameroon defender, followed immediately by an equaliser, set up the game for a grand finish.

But it was not to go South Africa's way and Cameroon scored their second goal just three minutes from full time, winning the match 2–1.

The final game was played at the FNB Stadium, Soccer City, south of Johannesburg. The teams were level at one each in the series, and this game was to be the decider. You could feel the tension as thousands – 65,000 stated as the official attendance number – made their way to the venue. Neither team disappointed, not least the South Africans. Twice they came from behind to draw level: first, Phil Masinga just before the end of the first half, followed by his cousin, Bennet Masinga, early in the second half. Final score: South Africa 2, Cameroon 2.

South Africa's passionate performance against Cameroon immediately sparked calls for an official team name. It had to be something that would serve not only as a praise name but also a cry to battle, and to cheer on the players on the pitch. The enthusiastic shouts of '*Shaya bafana, shaya!*' and '*Banyanyeng bafana, banyanyeng!*' heard during those first games continued to ring in fans' ears. Both phrases mean 'Thrash them boys, thrash them!' and so, when senior *Sowetan* sports journalists Molefi Mika, Sello Rabothata and Sibusiso Mseleku suggested 'Bafana Bafana', it seemed a fitting name.

Yet it caused quite a storm. The phrase is steeped in township

161

lingo and many found the literal definition of the words belittling, as 'bafana' literally means 'small boys'. Two major newspapers with predominantly white readership ran competitions to find what they believed would be an appropriate name. One came up with the name Golden Foxes, while a reader of a Sunday newspaper suggested the name Zebras, clearly not aware that Botswana's national team is known as the Zebras.

Mika later explained: 'It was clearly a case of not being familiar with black sport and culture. Whites often shout "What a boykie!"[113] when a rugby player excels, but this hardly belittles the player. Indeed, the term 'bafana' is often used in black African culture. The African cultural music group Ladysmith Black Mambazo is known as "Abafana base Mnambithi", which translates to "the boys from Ladysmith". Lamontville Golden Arrows are known as "Abafana be'sthende" (the back heel boys).'[114]

The name Bafana Bafana was adopted and endorsed by the Parliamentary Sports Committee in 1994. It was only at that point that the two newspapers abandoned their name search.

Following the victory of the Springboks in the 2007 Rugby World Cup, however, former president, Thabo Mbeki, reignited the furore when he said that soccer administrators should consider changing the name of the team. 'These are young people who carry the national colours, the pride and hopes of the nation. I really think we need to revisit names like that. The nation must feel proud, that we identify with these names. Bafana Bafana cannot have such meaning,' he said.[115]

Although some administrators supported the call, the opposition was overwhelming. The commercial value of the name was soon evident. As it turned out an enterprising entrepreneur had registered the Bafana Bafana trademark before SAFA could. In an ensuing court case, it was determined that SAFA could not claim sole and exclusive rights to the name and a bemused national association was forced to negotiate with the entrepreneur. Despite the controversy, the name Bafana Bafana endures and has been accepted by the majority of fans.

The new South African team had been given an unusually tight match schedule to mark their return to international soccer and, following the passionate performance against Cameroon, South African fans believed that Bafana Bafana could beat any of their African counterparts.

There were high expectations when the team took on Zimbabwe at the National Stadium in Harare in an Africa Cup of Nations qualifier in August 1992 – the boys' first away game since readmission. Yet the hopes were shattered when Vitalis Takawira, Rahman Gumbo and Peter Ndlovu hit the net – Ndlovu twice – compared to the single strike by Ewee Khambule for Bafana. Zimbabwean fans mocked the South African team – specifically Doctor Khumalo who they called a 'nurse' owing to his poor performance – and declared that the South Africans had overrated themselves.

More agony was to follow. Two weeks later Zambia beat Bafana 1–0 in another Africa Cup of Nations qualifying match, during which Phil Masinga was sent off. In a World Cup qualifier against Nigeria a few weeks later, South Africa were again thrashed 4–0. By then it had dawned on local soccer fans that the standard of South African soccer was still low and the impact of isolation was being felt. Cynical fans soon began to call the team the 4x4s, referring to the four-goal defeats to both Zimbabwe and Nigeria.

In response, Tshabalala was sacked as coach and replaced by Shakes Mashaba, who only had two weeks after the Nigerian defeat to prepare the team for a game against Congo. Fortunately,

Phil Masinga ensured a much desired victory for Bafana. Even though few would discuss this, this team included more white players than ever before – Steve Crowley, Mike Rowbotham, Neil Tovey and George Dearnaley.

Mashaba's replacement of Tshabalala was the first instalment of the high coach turnover that soon became a regular occurrence in the team's management set-up. By early 1993 yet another coach had been appointed, namely former Peruvian international Augusto Palacios. Under his direction Bafana achieved mixed success, but after Mexico thrashed South Africa 4–0, he also got the boot.

Clive Barker, who had coached several league teams since the early seventies, was appointed as coach in 1994. His credentials looked good and he was tasked to prepare the national squad for the upcoming 1996 Africa Cup of Nations. In their first game under Barker, Bafana beat Zimbabwe 1–0 in a friendly match, courtesy of yet another strike by Phil Masinga. Although Barker brought in new players like Edward Motale, Andrew Tucker, Eric Tinkler, Linda Buthelezi, Marks Maponyane and Wade du Plessis, he built a strong core around existing players in the squad – Masinga, Doctor Khumalo, Neil Tovey and others – perhaps contributing to him becoming South Africa's longest-serving and, according to match statistics, probably most successful coach.

Despite a few ups and downs, Barker's Boys beat Egypt in 1995 for the first time when they scored a famous victory in the Four Nations Cup. Incidentally, the Egyptians were then coached by Ruud Krol, who took up the coaching position at Orlando Pirates fifteen years later.

Bafana Bafana were ready for the Africa Cup of Nations, which the country was to host in January 1996 because the original hosts, Kenya, were not ready. Bafana proceeded to the semi-finals where they beat Ghana 3–0, thanks to two strikes by John 'Shoes' Moshoeu and another by Shaun Bartlett. Watched by a 75,000-strong partisan crowd, Bafana beat Tunisia 2–0 (both goals by Mark Williams) to become the 1996 Africa Cup of Nations champions.

Having conquered Africa, Bafana Bafana embarked on a new mission: '*Siyaya eFrance*' (we are going to France). The country qualified for the 1998 FIFA World Cup with a spectacular goal by Phil Masinga from 45 metres out to beat Congo 1–0. After being in charge for 43 games – 22 wins and nine draws – Barker resigned as coach in 1997 when SAFA refused to bow to his salary demand.

Although Bafana Bafana achieved much success against African teams, they always came unstuck against opposition from outside of the continent. In the run-up to the 1998 World Cup, they lost in several friendlies to England, Netherlands, Germany and Brazil.

The national squad bounced from one coach to another – three in one year – after Barker's resignation. Jomo Sono was called in to prepare the team for the Africa Cup of Nations to be held in Burkina Faso in 1998. During the tournament they held Angola goalless in the first game, drew 1–1 with Ivory Coast and, thanks to spectacular goals from a young Benni McCarthy against Namibia, Morocco and the Democratic Republic of Congo, again reached the finals. They lost 0–2 to the Pharaos.

Sono was replaced by Frenchman Phillipe Troussier. Buoyed by Bafana's success in qualifying for the 1998 World Cup, South African soccer fans perhaps pitched their expectations far too high. The disappointment when Bafana bombed out in the first round of the tournament was palpable. Troussier had to make way for Trott Moloto.

Moloto's appointment, which came after several calls from fans and some of the media to return to local coaches, brought a period of reasonable coaching stability. However, despite initial successes, defeats against the USA (4–0), Mexico (4–2), and a scrappy 1–0 win against Malta in 2000 cost him his job and he was relegated to senior assistant coach to Carlos Queiroz.

Queiroz did not last either and was fired after just two years. Shakes Mashaba, April Phumo and Stuart Baxter all followed in quick succession, but none lasting more than two years. Baxter, a relatively unknown ex-England under-18 and under-19 coach, particularly suffered under the media's wrath, with the *Sowetan* especially strident in its calls for his departure before he even had a chance to prove himself.

South Africa's coaching woes continued as Romanian Ted Dumitru took the team to the 2006 Africa Cup of Nations, where the team failed to score even a single goal. They also failed to qualify for the 2006 FIFA World Cup in Germany. Pitso Mosimane was appointed as interim coach until Brazilian Carlos Alberto Parreira took over the reins. Yet the downward spiral continued and analysts probed the administration for the malaise that has caused Bafana's continued lack of performance.

Former Kaizer Chiefs and Orlando Pirates coach, Joe Frickelton, has been scathing in his attacks on South African officials for the manner in which they have handled the coaching of Bafana Bafana. 'The only thing the poor coach in charge of Bafana is sure to collect is a barrage of knives in his back from misguided officials and members of the media who know less about the game than a char lady,' Frickelton reportedly said and added that 'not even the celebrated Jose Mourinho could save Bafana Bafana'.[116] While this assessment sounds harsh, the fact that Bafana has had eighteen coaches since 1992 perhaps justifies Frickelton's statement.

In a controversial move, Parreira resigned owing to the ill-health of his wife – or perhaps he realised that coaching Bafana was a hopeless cause. Countryman Joel Santana was appointed as replacement to take Bafana to the 2010 World Cup, following a recommendation by Parreira. It was a controversial appointment. SAFA justified it by saying that they needed continuity from the work Parreira had done, which Parreira believed Santana would be able to provide as he had a similar coaching philosophy.

Santana, however, did not endear himself to either South African fans or coaches of local teams. Coaches like Gordon Ingesund and Gavin Hunt had given up trying to offer advice,[117] as Santana prefered to have his countryman, Jairo Leal, as senior assistant coach. He knew very few of the PSL teams' players and soccer writers believe the contribution by Pitso Mosimane, the local coach who was a junior assistant, was ignored. Santana also did not speak English and communication with players and the media was difficult.

He repeatedly told the media that he had a plan and called on South Africans to give him a chance. After a game in which Bafana dominated possession for the entire game and still lost against a second-string Northern Ireland in September 2009, the fans – and SAFA – had clearly lost patience.

Santana resigned in late 2009, after which SAFA announced the reappointment of Parreira as national coach. As a sop to those who stridently called for the appointment of a local coach, the national association also announced that they planned to appoint SuperSport United coach Gavin Hunt to manage Bafana immediately after the World Cup.

The disappointing performance at international level raises the question whether South Africa is using all the available talent in the country. There has, for example, been a decline in the number of white players at the highest level, and players of Indian origin, who used to grace our soccer fields and played starring roles in the growth of soccer in the country, have all but disappeared.

And so it was back to the drawing board for South Africa only months before the 2010 World Cup. The country experienced a miracle in its political transformation; the hope lives on that another will happen.

11

The quest for the Cup

At first, we dreamt that one day South Africa would be a
non-racial, democratic society. Then, as sports fans,
that one day South Africa would be a member of FIFA,
after being expelled in 1976. And, finally, we dreamt
that the country would host the World Cup one day.
That dream has now been fulfilled and I feel blessed
to have been able to help make this happen.

DANNY JORDAAN[118]

It was October 1998. SAFA had received a circular from FIFA
inviting interested national associations to submit bids to host
the 2006 FIFA World Cup.

Only one African country, Morocco, had previously submitted bids to host one of the world's greatest sporting spectacles.
Despite being just a few hours by plane from Europe, which
they certainly banked on for getting them support from European federations, they failed at both their previous attempts.
They were to try again, but did not bargain on the fierce competition from the new kids on the African soccer block.

SAFA immediately put together a team to explore the possibility of successfully hosting a World Cup tournament in South
Africa. Danny Jordaan, former soccer player and politician, led
the group. The team had to report back in time for SAFA to
meet the 31 December deadline FIFA set for declaring interest

in organising the 2006 edition of the event. After several frantic telephone calls to test the waters, the team was convinced by the end of October that they would be able to muster enough support for South Africa to host the tournament. 'It's a go!' they reported back to SAFA.

By 31 December 1998 six federations had declared interest in hosting the 2006 FIFA World Cup, three of them from Africa. The African countries were South Africa, Nigeria and Morocco. Brazil, England and Germany were the other interested federations.

Jordaan, together with the SAFA team and an official Bid Committee, got down to working out strategies and timelines. The next critical date for South Africa would be 30 April of the following year, when the interested countries had to submit a comprehensive presentation to confirm their commitment to the bid process. And so began the quest for hosting the 2006 FIFA World Cup.

FIFA requested interested federations to submit their bid documents, prepared according to a list of requirements they sent out earlier, by the middle of August 1999. At the same time, Jordaan and his team had to convince government leaders and other stakeholders of the value of staging the World Cup, as FIFA would require government guarantees for granting the rights to stage the tournament. The South African team submitted their bid documents on time.

When the FIFA inspection delegates and ad hoc committee arrived in the country to view and assess the country's general infrastructure and facilities for the tournament, excitement began to build up in South African soccer. It was beginning to happen.

During the short time back in the international sporting world, South Africa had gained much experience in staging big international sports events: the Rugby World Cup in 1995, the Africa Cup of Nations soccer tournament in 1996 and being chosen as hosts for the 2003 Cricket World Cup. The response from the inspection delegation was positive: much still needed to be done, but there was nothing that would make it impossible for the country to stage the world contest.

But the ad hoc committee played their cards close to their chest, and South Africa had to wait till July 2000 to clear the last hurdle.

The hard work had only just begun and the lobbying continued furiously. The horse trading started. The federations from which Jordaan lobbied support sought the quid pro quo of support in the event they themselves had to bid for the spectacle. They seized every opportunity – conferences, seminars, meetings and local federation tournaments – to seek support for South Africa's bid. He invoked the Madiba magic – photo opportunities with Mandela were high on the agenda of federation officials – and many would have paid a fortune to get a photograph with him.

The response was varied: yes, perhaps, maybe, we'll think about it. If all the certain 'yes' votes were cast as promised, the bid committee reckoned South Africa should win the rights to the 2006 FIFA World Cup.

There were great expectations all round as the South African delegation left for Zurich, where the announcement would be made, in July 2000. For two days – 5 and 6 July – the country was on tenterhooks. Three days before the ballots were to be cast, Brazil withdrew its bid, leaving South Africa, Germany, England and Morocco to slug it out. It was a tight contest and required three rounds of voting. Morocco, garnering the fewest votes in the first round, was eliminated, followed by England in the second round. Only South Africa and Germany were left. It seemed at this point that the ballot would go to a casting vote – South Africa and Germany had each won eleven votes in the second round – if the voting patterns continued. South Africa also knew that they had the support – and most likely the vote – of FIFA President Sepp Blatter if it came to him having to use his casting vote.

But it was not to be. The delegate from Oceania, Charles Dempsey, whose mandate had been to vote for South Africa, abstained in the final round, and Germany beat South Africa by twelve votes to eleven. The outcome was later described by the local media as the 'Shame of Dempsey' and there were even (unproven) allegations of bribery. Dempsey himself had later cited 'intolerable pressure' for his decision to go against his federation's mandate. He gave no further detail, leaving a web of speculation, and might well have taken his secret to his grave.

After the almost overwhelming disappointment, Danny Jordaan and his team valiantly decided to start all over again. Mission 2010 FIFA World Cup began as soon as the go-ahead had been given by SAFA and the government. But another major setback to South Africa's credibility for hosting such an international soccer event was yet to come.

It was midweek in April 2001. A crazed atmosphere, generated by a game that had produced more edge than any other in the country recently, enveloped Johannesburg. There was no particular reason why this clash specifically should have had the edge it did. Over the years crowds at Orlando Pirates–Kaizer Chiefs derbies had shrunk, mostly because other teams had become equally competitive. But this was the kind of excitement associated with a Pirates–Chiefs clash.

The venue for this Bucs–Chiefs encounter was Ellis Park in

Johannesburg. This was unusual, for in the past the major derbies – Pirates versus Chiefs or Swallows – took place at Orlando Stadium. But Orlando Stadium had been neglected by the owners, the Soweto Council, and lost its allure to host big games.

Judged by the flags of the two teams fluttering on taxis and excited fans waving still more through the windows of cars and taxis, the game seemed to have generated an extraordinary amount of interest. This was quite surprising, as the outcome would not significantly have affected the log standings of the teams. The media had, for the first time in many years, succeeded in creating the kind of hype and expectation that is known to fill up stadiums.

At 18:10 local radio station Metro FM started its Sports Centre programme with the popular Chiefs song *Ha le so bone mathata!* (You have not seen trouble yet!). Listener calls to the programme were interspersed with the song, almost like a theme song. The debate raged: Chiefs fans called in to claim that it would be their day, while Pirates argued the opposite. Great soccer expectations hung over the region and those who had not planned to go to the stadium could well have decided that it was something they dared not miss.

As the fans converged in an almost pincer movement on the Ellis Park Stadium, it became clear that there were far more people than could be accommodated. Some fans had driven from as far as Swaziland and KwaZulu-Natal and were not going to be denied the opportunity to get into the stadium.

Officials decided that the game should start at the stipulated time, even though fans were still relentlessly trying to enter the stadium. The cheers and oohs and aahs, accompanied by the din of the vuvuzelas, only served to stir up the impatience of the fans outside. And then it happened.

One wave of fans surged forward, pushing against those in front. Irrational from frustration, fans just kept pushing, trampling over anything – and anyone – in their path. At the end of the stampede, 43 limp bodies were carried onto the pitch and it was later reported that close to 160 people were injured, 89 of them hospitalised.

The lyrics of the Chiefs song that had blared out of the radio studio earlier turned out to be ominous. Chiefs and Pirates chairmen, Kaizer Motaung and Irvin Khoza, stood forlorn, shocked, in the centre of the pitch as they surveyed the consequence of what was probably one moment of madness by someone, or a group. From the centre line, they appealed to fans to observe, in African tradition, the tragedy that had befallen soccer – and the nation. Thousands sat stunned, others hardly able to fully comprehend the enormity of what had happened.

News of the tragedy flashed around the world. A soccer tragedy almost always makes worldwide headline news, but for South Africa it was a disaster in more ways than one – it could well impact the country's bid for the 2010 World Cup. The initial stunned silence was followed by anger after allegations that tickets for the game had been oversold. Soon it raised issues about security and the suitability of the country's stadiums to host major games.

It was not the first time that over-eagerness and perhaps unwavering support for their team spurred fans to violent behaviour. In 1962 eleven fans were killed at the Jeppe Railway Station following a match between Moroka Swallows and Orlando Pirates at the Natalspruit Indian Sports Grounds. Although the event took place away from the stadium, it was clear that a game of the magnitude of the Soweto derby could not be planned in isolation of the transport requirements. The crush in the rush for transport carries the potential for an explosion at the

best of times, but even more so in the charged emotions following a soccer game.

Several games at township stadiums, and particularly at the
Orlando Stadium, previously had to be abandoned owing to
riotous fans storming onto the pitch to disrupt a game. In most
cases the riot would be sparked by fans who had laid bets on
the outcome of the game and would then lead a pitch invasion
if the game did not go in their favour. Referees were often assaulted and had to run for their lives – with players following
suit. As early as 1940 a referee was killed at the BMSC – the
first recorded incident of a fatal attack on a referee in South
Africa.

Another trick for the team on the losing end was to kick the
ball into their fans' area, where it would be knifed and, hiss-
ing its life away, be hurled back onto the field. The game would
usually end because no other ball would be available. Referees
who felt threatened and believed they might be attacked after
the game would position themselves, strategically, away from
the fans of the losing side, blow the final whistle and dash in
among the winning side's supporters for protection.

In January 1991 another derby between archrivals Orlando
Pirates and Kaizer Chiefs resulted in a riot in which 41 fans
died at the Oppenheimer Stadium in Orkney. Once more, poor
crowd management and planning were to blame for the riot.

Hardly a month after the Ellis Park tragedy, three more such
incidents rocked African soccer, the worst being the one in
Ghana's Accra Stadium, which left more than 120 fans dead.
This incident was sparked by fans throwing bottles and other
missiles onto the pitch. The police, instead of trying to manage
the crowd, responded with teargas. Thousands of fans panicked
and tried to make their way out of the stadium.

Afro-pessimists, who had never been in favour of the World

Cup being granted to an African country, used the Ellis Park tragedy as an opportunity to trash South Africa's credibility. FIFA tried to calm the outcry, stressing that, despite always having urged associations to tighten control and security at soccer games, several countries – not just in Africa – had failed to implement the recommended safety and security measures.

After the Ellis Park disaster, FIFA president, Sepp Blatter, would not discuss the potential impact the event could have on the chances of an African country hosting the World Cup tournament, saying instead that the priority had to be 'to obtain complete and exhaustive findings by the competent authorities on the causes of this latest tragedy in our game, so that lessons can be drawn for the future.' Football had to do 'everything in its power to ensure that such disasters [would] not occur again'.[119]

South Africa had to pick up its head and try for the honour of hosting the World Cup once more, this time aiming for the rights to 2010. Following the 2006 voting debacle, Sepp Blatter made a breakthrough when he convinced his executive of the need to introduce a new rotation policy that would give Africa a chance to host the World Cup. Germany was expected to stage a great tournament in 2006 and many wondered whether an African country would be able to match their standard. Blatter was confident that Africa would not disappoint and FIFA agreed to grant the continent its chance.

Jordaan and his team grasped the new opportunity. They knew that some European federations might still prefer a North African country for the 2010 World Cup, being much closer to reach than a destination thousands of kilometres southwards.

Not surprisingly, Libya and Tunisia (joint bid), Egypt and Morocco also saw this as their opportunity. Morocco had in fact been there before and had the experience of presenting World Cup bids. Was this their time?

Jordaan, together with Irvin Khoza and other executives of both SAFA and the PSL, got working. It was now or not in our lifetime for South Africa. A new round of horse trading began: Brazil would support South Africa if South Africa supported their bid for the 2014 edition in turn. Libya and Tunisia's bid was rejected as FIFA decided not to entertain co-hosting following the Korea–Japan experiment. Tunisia subsequently withdrew its bid, while Libya was not considered because alone the country fell short on the stipulations set out in the FIFA requirements document. This left Egypt, Morocco and South Africa to battle it out. It would come down to the one that could muster the strongest support.

During the lobbying for the rights to the 2006 World Cup, Danny Jordaan had made many friends – some fair-weather, but others genuine, no doubt. One such friend was to prove crucial to South Africa's bid. Former Union of European Football Association's (UEFA) president, Lennart Johansson, had promised Jordaan that he would lobby for South Africa. The Swede is believed to have led the UEFA rally behind South Africa, getting the support of at least six of his colleagues on the FIFA executive to vote for the country.

The voting margin – fourteen to the ten for Morocco – showed how crucial his support was. I caught up telephonically with Jordaan once more, just as he prepared to go to a meeting in Denmark that Johansson would also be attending. I could sense the urgency in his voice and he only had time to say a few words before he had to dash off. At the meeting Johansson, battling to hold back tears, told Jordaan, 'I promised you that I would help you to bring the World Cup to Africa in 2010, and I did.' It clearly was the action of a genuine friend.

Johansson truly believed that Africa deserved at least this chance to stage the World Cup and in a report from Denmark stated: 'The time for Africa is now. This is the world's biggest event and it will benefit the people of South Africa from every point of view – from tourism to retail spend, to the pride it will give your people as images of your country are beamed to more than 200 countries around the world.' [120]

'Thank you for helping us make our dream come true,' an equally emotional Jordaan responded.

By 15 May 2004 Jordaan had been on the World Cup road for just over five years. When Sepp Blatter opened 'that' envelope in Zurich, the rafters of the Dolder Grand Hotel reverberated. A tear rolled down Mandela's wrinkled cheek. He had also given the first bid his full support, but this time the Madiba talisman had worked its magic. This was a victory for all the people of Africa. 'For ordinary people in the street, the unemployed, those without food, the award of this World Cup has given them hope,' Jordaan said at a press conference.

'The credit [for being awarded the 2010 FIFA World Cup] is for Nelson Mandela. Madiba struggled for a free and democratic South Africa, a South Africa that can compete equally with the best in the world – a country of hope for a better and brighter future. When we host a successful 2010 FIFA World Cup, I hope Tata Madiba will look back and come to the conclusion that his efforts, his travels and contributions were not in vain,' Jordaan added.[121]

Jordaan spent almost all his life involved in community service. He was a member of the South African Students Organisation (SASO), which, under leaders like Steve Biko and Onkgopotse Tiro, first challenged the exclusive structure of student bodies at tertiary institutions. He trained as a teacher and was actively involved in civic politics in the Eastern Cape through the United Democratic Front and later also as an ANC Member of Parliament in the first democratic government.

After being appointed as Chief Executive Officer of SAFA in 1997, Jordaan worked hard to transform the organisation into a viable soccer federation committed to all the principles, especially non-racialism in sport, for which he had fought so hard. He put all his negotiation skills to use during the process of rebuilding SAFA, which had been running at a loss and had to be bailed out to the tune of R4 million by Irvin Khoza. The challenge for Jordaan had been to turn around the revenue status of the federation, which he achieved with distinction.

As the fortunes of professional soccer in South Africa grew, so, too, did the stature of SAFA. Some would argue that this growth happened to the detriment of amateur soccer, as SAFA seemed to focus on the national team, Bafana Bafana, while regional structures around the country collapsed and in some cases exist in all but name.

At the executive elections in 2009, the organisation was plunged into controversy when Molefi Oliphant announced that he would not stand for re-election, and both strong-men of South African soccer, Irvin Khoza and Jordaan, announced their candidature. Khoza, as chairman of the PSL, is a vice-president of SAFA, while Jordaan is a former CEO of SAFA.

Their candidature was challenged on technicalities and both withdrew their nominations to clear the way for the election of Kirsten Nematandani, who was duly elected unopposed – with some regions claiming this process was flawed, and the PSL threatening not to recognise the new executive.

Getting hold of Jordaan is any journalist's nightmare, but when I eventually managed to pin him down to check on information for this book, he demonstrated the one quality that many other administrators lack – the ability to interact with journalists. He started off the conversation with light banter, asking me: 'So, you are among the journalists who do not believe that I played soccer?'

Jordaan had indeed played provincial soccer and cricket in the Eastern Cape and there are many who remember his dashing runs down the wings. We both laughed it off, and I asked him whether he considers himself a star of the SASF. It was all still said in jest – not only did Jordaan play in the Fed, as the SASF was also known, he was also president of the Border region of that organisation.

'The problem with you journalists is that you believe that soccer administrators are usually failed players!' he said jokingly, referring to the oft stated view that when players fail as players, they turn to administration to pursue their passion.

Nothing had quite prepared him for the fast-paced life his being in charge of South Africa's World Cup bid would bring. Once the decision had been taken to bid for the FIFA World Cup, he began a life he himself has described as living out of a suitcase, in hotel rooms and on long-haul flights. In a radio interview he recalled how he once only had time to change suitcases at the Johannesburg airport after arriving on a morning flight from South America, before having to depart again later the same day to another destination in the East. He became a stranger to his wife and family.

After the successful bid campaign, Jordaan repeatedly emphasised in public that winning the bid was but the first step in a long journey of hard work over the coming six years. Stadiums were to be built or upgraded, public transport matters and road infrastructure had to be addressed, security issues were to be considered, sufficient accommodation facilities had to be provided for. The South African government committed to support the Local Organising Committee all the way.

Yet cynical remarks from both outside and inside the country were often heard during the following years. Despite reassurance from FIFA that the tournament would only be moved to another country in the event of a natural disaster and that it was standard practice for them to have a contingency plan for such an eventuality, rumours that South Africa would not be ready in time continued to dog preparations. There were even reports in Germany that some FIFA executives were doubtful as to whether South Africa would be able to host the World Cup, suggesting the United States should stage the tournament instead; others proposed that the tournament should rather be hosted in Germany once more.

But FIFA were convinced of their decision and stressed that Sepp Blatter has spent years ensuring the event goes to Africa. Why would they want to take the event elsewhere, when FIFA has invested in setting up an office and stationing several FIFA employees in South Africa and had invited more than 60 South African officials to FIFA observer programmes at the Germany tournament in 2006?

South Africa was determined to keep to its commitments and undertakings. Several projects to improve public transport facilities and road infrastructure were launched. Match venues were also improved. Seven existing stadiums that form part of the group of ten host venues were substantially upgraded, while three new venues were built.[122] Construction projects in preparation for the event provided a substantial economic injection, especially in light of the prevailing worldwide economic downturn.

The new Green Point Stadium in Cape Town may be one of the most scenic stadiums in South Africa, with the welcoming waters of the Atlantic Ocean within earshot and the world-renowned Table Mountain as backdrop.

The Moses Mabhida Stadium in Durban was designed through public competition and, according to the winning consortium, the design was inspired by the South African flag and the history it represents: the two legs of the arch merging into one symbolises the unity of a nation that was once so divided.

At a ceremony to celebrate the completion of the iconic arch spanning over the stadium early in 2009, provincial premier Sbu Ndebele said that the arch is not only an architectural and engineering masterpiece, but also an icon that symbolises and spans years of history, years of hope and years of work. It serves as testimony to the spirit that has presided in South Africa since being awarded the games.[123]

'As host of the 2010 FIFA World Cup, South Africa stands not as a country alone, but rather as a representative of Africa, and as part of an African family of nations, 'he declared.[124]

His words echoed those of Jordaan, who previously acknowledged the support of CAF members at the CAF Assembly in Lagos in February 2009. 'South Africa is a proud 2010 host, but we are simply the custodians of the tournament on behalf of African football. The 2010 FIFA World Cup will be a tribute to all that is great about African football. We will have facilities that compare to the best in the world, but what will set this FIFA World Cup apart will be an unforgettable explosion of colour, music, rhythm, dance and joy. The unbelievable passion and spirit of African football fans and players are unmatched,' Jordaan said.[125]

The sentiment was aptly summed up by Togolese Emmanuel Adebayor during his acceptance speech at the 2008 African Footballer of the Year ceremony held in Nigeria early in 2009: 'As a unit, as a family, we can achieve. We must believe.'[126]

South Africa hosted a successful Confederations Cup at four of the 2010 World Cup venues in June 2009. The tournament was won by Brazil, but not before both they and Spain had endured nail-biting games, courtesy of Bafana Bafana. Although South Africa, as host nation, automatically qualified for the tournament, their performance in the Confederations Cup assured fans – and opposition – that they are not only in the World Cup to add to the numbers, but to compete.

There is no doubt that Africa's first FIFA World Cup will turn out to be a celebration of continental football unity and achievement, and fans from across the continent are sure to use this opportunity to make the games a success.

The preparatory work is done; now for the Cup. South Africa is ready – and so is the African continent. In the words of Danny Jordaan: 'The dream is reality, the game is on.'[127]

Endnotes

1   *World* was previously known as *Bantu World*, founded in 1932. The name changed during the 1950s.

2   'Bra' is a term used as form of respect in township language. It is an abbreviation of 'brother' and sometimes also spelt 'Bro', although this spelling is not generally used in the townships.

3   The terms 'witchdoctor' and sangoma are often used interchangeably, but traditionally the former refers to a person who professes to be able to cast spells – usually evil – while the latter refers to a person who uses herbs to cure people from diseases or evil spirits. The Zulu term inyanga often refers to either, but directly translated means 'doctor'.

4   Cited in Alegi, P. *Laduma! Soccer, politics and society in South Africa*. Scotsville, South Africa: University of KwaZulu-Natal Press, 2004, p. 49.

5   Maguire, R. The People's Club: a social and institutional history of Orlando Pirates Football Club, 1937–1973. BA Honours dissertation, University of the Witwatersrand, Johannesburg, 1991.

6   Callers phoned in to *Sports Centre*, a sports programme hosted by Robert Marawa on Metro FM, weekdays from 18:00–19:30.

7   Martin, P. as cited in Alegi, P. Katanga vs Johannesburg: a history of the first sub-Saharan African football championship. *African Historical Review* [formerly *Kleio*] 31, 1999, pp. 55–74.

8   Alegi, P. Katanga vs Johannesburg: a history of the first sub-Saharan African football championship. *African Historical Review* [formerly *Kleio*] 31, 1999, 55–74.

9   Ibid.

10 *Witch doctors placated*, BBC Sport, 6 April 2002. Available from http://news.bbc.co.uk/sport2/hi/football/africa/1914853.stm# [Accessed 26 October 2009].

11 Khashane, F. Personal interview, May 2009. Khashane was shot and killed two months later in Soweto in an armed robbery.

12 McAravey, C. Personal interview, May 2009.

13 Dearnaley, G. Personal interview, January 2009.

14 Usuthu was a feared regiment of soldiers under Zulu King Cetshwayo. The term is often used to refer to AmaZulu.

15 Kortjaas, B. The white boy flushed with success in a black league. *Sunday Times*, 23 August 2009, p. 8. Available from www.timeslive.co.za/sport/article33823.ece [Accessed 26 October 2009].

16 *Soccer Laduma* claims to be the biggest soccer publication in Africa. The column is called 'Still in touch with...'.

17 Still in touch with Ronnie Zondi. 2009. *Soccer Laduma*, 2 September 2009.

18 *Footballers held for practising witchcraft*, Zeenews.com, 6 October 2008. Available from www.zeenews.com/news474451.html [Accessed 26 October 2009].

19 History of football: the origins. FIFA.com. Available from www.fifa.com/classicfootball/history/game/historygame1.html [Accessed 26 October 2009].

20 History of football: Britain, the home of football. FIFA.com. Available from www.fifa.com/classicfootball/history/game/historygame2.html [Accessed 26 October 2009].

21 Alegi, P. *Laduma! Soccer, politics and society in South Africa*, p. 15.

22 South Africa was one of the first countries to found its own football association. This was well ahead of similar associations in the Netherlands and Denmark (1889), New Zealand (1891), Argentina (1893) and Italy (1898). In 1896 the Transvaal Indian Football Association became the first black football association in South Africa.

23 The team was founded in 1906 by a Mr Scotts from Nyasaland and clerical staff from the colonial government, THD Ngcobo, AJ Ndlhovu, and Kanys Ntombela.

24 Alegi, P. *Laduma! Soccer, politics and society in South Africa*, p. 25.

25 Alegi, P. Sport, race and liberation before apartheid: a preliminary study of Albert Luthuli, 1920s–1952s. South African History Online Library. Available from www.sahistory.org.za/pages/library-resources/articles_papers/sports-race-liberation.htm [Accessed 26 October 2009].

26 Luthuli, A., *Let my people go*. Cape Town: Tafelberg, 2006, p. 16.

27 Ibid., p. 23.

28 Ibid.

29 *Creative acts of social solidarity: social movements and the democratic state*. Kgalema Motlanthe in an address to a Centre for Urban and Built Environment Studies seminar on social movements, August 2004. Available from www.anc.org.za/show.php?doc=ancdocs/pubs/umrabulo/umrabulo21/creative_acts.html.

30 As cited in Alegi, P. *Laduma! Soccer, politics and society in South Africa*, p. 40.

31 This expression, as well as 'keeping the natives amused', was used quite liberally in white conversations and communications among white liberals. The two expressions are used in the same context and not necessarily attributed to any person in particular.

32 The monetary unit in South Africa was the South African pound until the country became a republic in 1961. South African rand replaced

the pound as the official monetary unit only in 1961, to coincide with South Africa becoming a republic.

33   Alegi, P. *Laduma! Soccer, politics and society in South Africa*, p. 30.

34   The black association gave this as one of the reasons for the need to charge admission at the gates for major games.

35   Kuper, L. *An African Bourgeoisie: race, class and politics in South Africa*. New Haven: Yale University Press, 1965, p. 347. Cited by Alegi, P. Entertainment, entrepreneurship and politics in South African football in the 1950s, a paper delivered for the WISER seminar series, University of the Witwatersrand, 23 August 2003. Available from http://wiserweb.wits.ac.za/PDF%20Files/wirs%20-%20alegi.PDF [Accessed 26 October 2009].

36   Alegi, P. Entertainment, entrepreneurship and politics in South African football in the 1950s, a paper delivered for the WISER seminar series, University of the Witwatersrand, 23 August 2003, p. 2. Available from http://wiserweb.wits.ac.za/PDF%20Files/wirs%20-%20alegi.PDF [Accessed 26 October 2009].

37   Alegi, P. *Laduma! Soccer, politics and society in South Africa*, p. 53.

38   Schlemmer, L. Article in *South Africa Review*, November 1991.

39   Badenhorst, CM. Mines, missionaries and the municipality: organised African sport and recreation in Johannesburg, c1920–1950. PhD thesis, University of Michigan, Ann Arbor, 1992.

40   Ibid.

41   Badenhorst CM. & Rogerson C.M. Teach the Native to play: social control and organised black sport on the Witwatersrand, 1920–1939. *Geojournal*, 12(2), 1986, pp. 197–202.

42   Badenhorst, CM. as cited by Odendaal, A. *The story of an African game*. Claremont: David Philip, 2003, p. 94.

43   Odendaal, A. *The story of an African game*, p. 94.

44   Badenhorst, CM. as cited by Nauright, J. *Sport, cultures and identities in South Africa*. London: Leicester University Press, 1997, p. 111.

45   Badenhorst, CM. Mines, missionaries and the municipality: organised African sport and recreation in Johannesburg, c1920–1950. PhD thesis, University of Michigan, Ann Arbor, 1992.

46   Alegi, P. Katanga vs Johannesburg: a history of the first sub-Saharan African football championship. *African Historical Review* [formerly *Kleio*] 31, 1999, p. 60.

47   *Khosi* is a Zulu word that means chief, ruler or king.

48   This is one of the oldest surviving professional clubs in South Africa.

49   Report on FIFA online. Available at www.fifa.com/confederationscup/news/newsid1073689.html [Accessed 26 October 2009].

50   FIFA Statutes state that discrimination of any kind against a country, private person or groups of people on account of ethnic origin, gender,

language, religion, politics or any other reason is strictly prohibited and punishable by suspension or expulsion.

51 Race Relations Survey, 1958: 9 as cited by Nauright, J. *Sport, culture and identities in South Africa*, p. 127.

52 Ibid.

53 Draper, M. Custom and policy – not law – bar mixed sport, *The Star,* 31 January 1963.

54 Malay says she loved the Verwoerd children, *Sunday Times*, 25 November 1973. Reproduced in *The Best of The Sunday Times – 100 Years. Celebrating the Best of the Paper for the People. Part 3: 1956–1981*, 2007.

55 Darby, P. *Africa, football and FIFA: politics, colonialism and resistance*. New York: Frank Cass, 2002. p. 73. See also Homberg, H. FIFA and the 'Chinese Question', 1954–1980: an exercise of statutes. *Historical Social Research*, 31(1), 2006, p. 72.

56 Furlong, WB. A bad week for Mr. B. *SI Vault*, 11 March 1968. Available from http://sportsillustrated.cnn.com/vault/article/magazine/MAG1080927/index.htm [Accessed 26 October 2009].

57 Minutes of FASA meeting, 2 March 1963.

58 Darby, P. *Africa, football and FIFA: politics, colonialism and resistance*, p. 74.

59 Ibid., pp. 74–76.

60 Many Third World countries could often not afford to send delegates to international sports congresses and so had to select carefully where they went within very tight budgets.

61 Letter from SABFA to FIFA, 10 January 1967.

62 Ibid.

63 Letter from Sir Stanley Rous (president of FIFA) to Bethuel Morolo, president of SABFA, 25 January 1967.

64 The Football Association of South Africa (FASA) was founded in 1892 as the South African Football Association.

65 Letter from Sir Stanley Rous (president of FIFA) to Bethuel Morolo, president of SABFA, 25 January 1967.

66 Badenhorst, CM. Mines, missionaries and the municipality: organised African sport and recreation in Johannesburg, c1920–1950. PhD thesis, University of Michigan, Ann Arbor, 1992.

67 This refers to a statement by Berge Phillips, president of the General Assembly of International Federations, that political, racial or religious ground should not interfere with sport policies.

68 *Football in South Africa: timeline*. South Afican History Online. Available from www.sahistory.org.za/pages/artsmediaculture/culture%20&%20heritage/sport/timeline.htm.

69 South Africa's chief propagandist for apartheid, Eschel Rhoodie, travelled the world for five years as the country's Secretary for Information. His

aim was to create a positive image of the country. His Information Ministry channelled millions of rands towards a 'dirty tricks' campaign through a slush fund created from tax payers' money. Rhoodie set up several projects, including buying the newspaper *Citizen* in South Africa and funnelling US$11 million into a failed effort to gain control of the now defunct *Washington Star.*

70 *Biography of R.F. Botha.* South African History Online. Available from www.sahistory.org.za/pages/people/bios/botha-p.htm.

71 Cited by United States Assistant Secretary of State, Richard Moose, during hearings on 'US policy toward South Africa' before the Subcommittees on International Economic Policy and Trade, on Africa, and on International Organisations of the Committee on Foreign Affairs, House of Representatives, 30 April 1980. Available from www.archive.org/stream/uspolicytowardso00unit/uspolicytowardso00unit_djvu.txt.

72 Carlin, J. *Playing the enemy. Nelson Mandela and the game that made a nation.* London: Atlantic Books, 2008, p. 4.

73 The name of this championship was later changed to the CAF Champions League.

74 Burton, ARE. *Cape Colony Today.* Cape Town: Townshend, Taylor & Snashall, 1909.

75 Nauright, J. *Sport, cultures and identities in South Africa.* London: Leicester University Press, 1997.

76 Schoggl, H. King, I. Johnson, M, statistics prepared for the Rec. Sport. Soccer Statistics Foundation. 1998/2008. This is supported by Nauright, J. citing Couzens and Parker.

77 Alegi, P. p. 106. See also endnote 108, p. 180.

78 Pretoria Methodist, quite ironically Bethuel Morolo's team, also played in a similar match a year earlier against the white team Texas Rangers. They beat them 9–0 at the Wemmer Sports Grounds in Johannesburg before the NEAD stepped in to warn the organisers that white teams were not allowed to play on NEAD grounds under any circumstances.

79 An interview with Paul Yule, director of *Not Cricket: The Basil D'Oliveira Conspiracy.* BBC Four. Available from www.bbc.co.uk/bbcfour/documentaries/features/not-cricket.shtml.

80 Minutes of th 61st session of the IOC held in Baden Baden, 16–20 November 1963.

81 Minutes of Fifth Biennial SACOS Conference, March 1983.

82 Booth, D. *The race game: sport and politics in South Africa.* London: Frank Cass, 1998, p. 156.

83 Ibid., p. 157.

84 Nauright, J. 'The Mecca of Native Scum' and a 'running sore of evil': white Johannesburg and the Alexandra Township Removal Debate, 1935–1945. *African Historical Review*, 30, 1998, p. 64.

85 Ibid., p. 65.

86 Open Africa Route. Available from http://www.openafrica.org/route/alexandra-township-of-rhythm-route.

87 A spaza shop is an informal convenience store, usually run out of the owner's home.

88 The South African rand replaced the South African pound as the official monetary unit only in 1961, to coincide with South Africa becoming a republic. Also see http://www.highlandsparkfc.co.za/history.html for more information regarding the history of Highlands Park.

89 Thousands of blacks were arrested because their passbooks were not in order owing to some technicality. Such people were sent to jail and to work on potato and other farms as cheap labour for the white farmers. They would be joined by hundreds who had been tricked into signing six-month contracts to work on the farms. Some died through the harshness of their exposure and ruthlessness of the farmers and would be buried on the farms in shallow graves dug by fellow prisoners, as warning to the consequences of not complying with the white bosses' orders. A potato boycott was launched following an exposé by activist Gert Sibande and journalists Ruth First and Joe Gqabi, and more effectively by 'Mr Drum' Henry Nxumalo and photographer Jurgen Schadeberg in *Drum* in the fifties. The South African Congress of Trade Unions distributed pamphlets that declared: 'If you eat a potato, you are eating the blood of a fellow worker who has been killed and buried on these farms.' First and Gqabi were both victims of the apartheid security machinery: First in Mozambique and Gqabi in Botswana. Nxumalo died mysteriously; his body was found dumped in the streets of Sophiatown.

90 Sampson, A. *Drum: an African adventure and afterwards.* London: Hodder & Stoughton, 1983.

91 Tragedy struck the SASL when eleven fans died at Jeppe Railway Station following a Swallows-Pirates game at the Natalspruit Indian Sports Grounds.

92 Minutes of SABFA Executive Committee, 24 January 1965.

93 Cited in Alegi, P. *Laduma! Soccer, politics and society in South Africa*, p. 132.

94 The use of the term 'non-racial' in the context of the SASL refers to the inclusion of Africans, Indians and Coloureds. Although the white teams had a principle of non-racialism they refused to participate, preferring to stay in their own exclusive league.

95 The league featured Kaizer Chiefs, Moroka Swallows Big XV, Orlando Pirates, Vaal Professionals, Pimville United Brothers, Real Katlehong City, Bantu Callies, Mamelodi United, Witbank Aces, Dalton Brothers, Lamontville Golden Arrows, Bloemfontein Celtic, Mangaung United and Zulu Royals. Major competitions included the Sales House Cup,

shared between Orlando Pirates, Chiefs and Moroka Swallows and Arcadia over its fifteen-year life, with the Ohlsonns Challenge being won in
its single edition by Swallows. The BP Top Eight, running from 1972 to
2008, with a three-year break between 1997 and 1999, was one of the
longest running competitions in the NPSL.

96   Mokone, S & Ryan, JW. *Kalamazoo! The life and times of a soccer player:
an autobiography*. Pretoria: De Jager–Haum, 1980.

97   An overseas soccer career is not always easy, as Albert 'Hurry Hurry'
Johanneson found after his nine-season spell with Leeds United. When
his career ended, Johanneson drowned his sorrows in alcohol and died
a lonely death in his apartment in 1995.

98   According to statistics by Transfer Markt. Available from http://www.
transfermarkt.co.uk/en/spieler/3091/benni-mccarthy/profil.html [Accessed
26 October 2009].

99   Gerhart, GM. & Karis, T (eds). *From protest to challenge: a documentary
history of African politics in South Africa: 1882–1964, Vol. 4: Political
Profiles*. Stanford, California: Hoover Institution Press, 1977.

100 History of Orlando Pirates. Available from http://www.orlandopiratesfc.
com/default.asp?cId = 5298 [Accessed 26 October 2009].

101 Khoza was made an honorary colonel by the South African Defence
Force in 2009.

102 Who is Irvin Khoza?. *BBC Sport*, 10 December 2004. Available from
http://news.bbc.co.uk/sport2/hi/football/africa/4085683.stm [Accessed on
26 October 2009].

103 *The history of Moroka Swallows football club*. Moroka Swallows. Available
from http://www.morokaswallows.co.za/content.asp?id = 16831 [Accessed
26 October 2009].

104 Motaung, K. Personal interview, Johannesburg, 2002.

105 *Stokvels* are social gatherings at which members contribute a fixed
amount of money every month into a group savings plan.

106 Ga-Rankuwa is a black township north of Pretoria, and was formerly
part of the Bantustan of Bophuthatswana.

107 Sono was named Jomo after Jomo (Burning Spear) Kenyetta.

108 Moripe, L. Personal interview, Atteridgeville, February 2009.

109 Ibid.

110 According to http://www.sahistory.org.za/pages/chronology/special-chrono/
society/sa-soccer.htm#1970 [Accessed 26 October 2009].

111 'Groovy' was a popular early canned cooldrink. It became a generic township reference to all canned cooldrinks.

112 The Africa Champions Cup tournament was later renamed to the CAF
Champions League.

113 The word 'boykie' means 'small boy'. It is popularly used in informal
conversation to show praise and approval.

114 Mika, M. Personal interview, November 2008.

115 Quoted by Eberl, N. *Why Bafana Bafana have to rebrand for 2010*. Available from www.bizcommunity.com/Article/196/147/19384.html [Accessed on 26 October 2009].

116 Sapa report on 14 October 2005 as published on www.news24.com

117 In an interview with Robert Marawa, Metro FM, 9 September 2009.

118 As quoted in Austin, S. *Is South Africa ready for 2010?* BBC Sport, 11 June 2009. Available from http://news.bbc.co.uk/sport2/hi/football/8088624.stm [Accessed on 26 October 2009].

119 Quist-Arcton, O. *Government orders full enquiry into soccer tragedy*. allAfrica.com, 11 April 2001. Available from http://allafrica.com/stories/200104120227.html [Accessed 26 October 2009].

120 Quoted in *Jordaan's emotional meeting with SA's biggest 2010 ally*, FIFA.com, 27 March 2009. Available from http://www.fifa.com/worldcup/news/newsid = 1041666.html [Accessed 26 October 2009].

121 Namanya, M. *Danny Jordaan delighted for South Africa, Mandela*. Monitor, 22 June 2009. Available from http://allafrica.com/stories/200906220187.html [Accessed 26 October 2009].

122 Of the thirteen venues initially proposed as World Cup venues, ten were eventually announced by FIFA in March 2006 (approximate capacities are shown in parentheses): Soccer City in Johannesburg (95,000); Moses Mabhida in Durban (70,000); Green Point in Cape Town (68,000); Ellis Park in Johannesburg (62,000); Loftus Versfeld in Pretoria (50,000); Nelson Mandela Bay in Port Elizabeth (48,000); Free State in Bloemfontein (48,000); Peter Mokaba in Polokwane (46,000); Mbombela in Nelspruit (44,000) and Royal Bafokeng in Rustenburg (42,000).

123 *Moses Mahbida Stadium – sheer magnificence!* KwaZulu-Natal 2010. Available from http://www.kzn2010.gov.za/node/29 [Accessed 26 October 2009].

124 As quoted in *Lights switched on at Durban's 2010 Stadium*, Architect Africa Online, 2 February 2009. Available from http://architectafrica.com/Moses-Mabhida-Stadium.

125 *United Africa Readies for 2010*. FIFA.com, 13 February 2009. Available from http://www.fifa.com/worldcup/news/newsid = 1026819.html [Accessed 26 October 2009].

126 Ibid.

127 As quoted in Austin, S. *Is South Africa ready for 2010?*, BBC Sport, 11 June 2009. Available from http://news.bbc.co.uk/sport2/hi/football/8088624.stm [Accessed 26 October 2009].